797,885 Books
are available to read at

Forgotten Books

www.ForgottenBooks.com

Forgotten Books' App
Available for mobile, tablet & eReader

ISBN 978-1-333-52183-7
PIBN 10514975

This book is a reproduction of an important historical work. Forgotten Books uses state-of-the-art technology to digitally reconstruct the work, preserving the original format whilst repairing imperfections present in the aged copy. In rare cases, an imperfection in the original, such as a blemish or missing page, may be replicated in our edition. We do, however, repair the vast majority of imperfections successfully; any imperfections that remain are intentionally left to preserve the state of such historical works.

Forgotten Books is a registered trademark of FB &c Ltd.
Copyright © 2015 FB &c Ltd.
FB &c Ltd, Dalton House, 60 Windsor Avenue, London, SW19 2RR.
Company number 08720141. Registered in England and Wales.

For support please visit www.forgottenbooks.com

1 MONTH OF FREE READING

at

www.ForgottenBooks.com

By purchasing this book you are eligible for one month membership to ForgottenBooks.com, giving you unlimited access to our entire collection of over 700,000 titles via our web site and mobile apps.

To claim your free month visit:

www.forgottenbooks.com/free514975

* Offer is valid for 45 days from date of purchase. Terms and conditions apply.

English
Français
Deutsche
Italiano
Español
Português

www.forgottenbooks.com

Mythology Photography **Fiction** Fishing Christianity **Art** Cooking Essays **Buddhism** Freemasonry Medicine **Biology** Music **Ancient Egypt** Evolution Carpentry Physics Dance Geology **Mathematics** Fitness Shakespeare **Folklore** Yoga Marketing **Confidence** Immortality Biographies Poetry **Psychology** Witchcraft Electronics Chemistry History **Law** Accounting **Philosophy** Anthropology Alchemy Drama Quantum Mechanics Atheism Sexual Health **Ancient History Entrepreneurship** Languages Sport Paleontology Needlework Islam **Metaphysics** Investment Archaeology Parenting Statistics Criminology **Motivational**

THE PHILOSOPHERS

AND

THE FRENCH REVOLUTION

BY

P. A. WADIA

PROFESSOR OF HISTORY AND POLITICAL ECONOMY,
GUJARAT COLLEGE, AHMEDABAD

LONDON
SWAN SONNENSCHEIN & CO., LIM.
HIGH STREET, BLOOMSBURY, W.C.
1904

A 187829

PREFACE

THIS small treatise is intended to tackle the question how far the eighteenth century writers in France can be made responsible, directly or indirectly, for the outbreak of the French Revolution, in whatever sense the term French Revolution is understood. In our times a halting attitude between two extremes has often been dubbed with the name of historic impartiality; it is just possible the emphatic attitude I have taken up in the following pages may not represent historic impartiality in that sense—may not even represent historic truth in the proper sense of the term. I will be satisfied if the stress I have laid on one side of the case leads to a further discussion of the question, and promotes the aims of history.

One thing more, and I will close the preface. It would be ungrateful of me not to recognise the valuable help I have received from Professor J. H. Muirhead throughout the publication of this work, and not to express my deep sense of obligation to him for his kindness.

GUJARAT COLLEGE, AHMEDABAD.

TABLE OF CONTENTS

THE PHILOSOPHERS AND THE FRENCH REVOLUTION

CHAP.		PAGE
I.	INTRODUCTORY	9
II.	NO REPUBLICAN PARTY EXISTED IN FRANCE UNDER THE ANCIEN RÉGIME	19
III.	REPUBLICAN IDEAS UNDER THE ANCIEN RÉGIME	36
IV.	THE CONTINUITY OF EUROPEAN HISTORY	44
V.	THE PHILOSOPHERS AN EVIDENCE OF THIS CONTINUITY—INDIVIDUALISM	51
VI	INDIVIDUALISM IN ETHICS AND POLITICS	66
VII.	REVOLUTIONARY AGITATION A PECULIAR TRAIT OF FRENCH HISTORY IN GENERAL	76
VIII.	FRENCH LITERATURE A REFLECTION OF FRENCH SOCIETY	95
IX.	CONCLUSION	124
	INDEX	129

The Philosophers and the French Revolution

CHAPTER I

INTRODUCTORY

No doctrine has been so often preached by writers of great weight, and often taught with such great eloquence, as that the Republic established in 1792 and its democratic organisation were the direct outcome of the philosophy of the eighteenth century, of the works of the literary group which had co-operated towards the publication of the Encyclopædia, and of the doctrines of the political philosophers who preceded the Revolutionary Era. Ever since Louis XVI., encountering the works of Voltaire and Rousseau in the library of the Order of Malta in the Temple, designated them the source of all his misfortunes, the opinion has widely prevailed that everything that happened in the course of the Revolution could be traced directly or indirectly to the writings of the eighteenth century

The growth of this opinion may even be traced back to the early sixties of the same century, when we find Palissot ending one of his comedies with the following lines: "At last all philosophy is banished from the house, and we have amongst us only honest men." The audience of the times, which felt offended at the lines quoted above, applauded the valet in the same play who, whilst stealing his master's property, exclaimed: "I am now a philosopher!" The preface to Palissot's comedy, sold in a clandestine fashion, gave the philosophers the appellations of rogues and rascals, and said that the Encyclopædia had become a matter of shame for the nation.[1] We are told that if about this time some inquisitive spirit had consulted the Court of France as to the causes of the fatal defeats at Rosbach and Minden, and of the ruin of the French fleet and the general disorganisation of affairs, he would have learnt that it was the new philosophy to which all these misfortunes were to be attributed, that it was this philosophy that had extinguished the military spirit, the unquestioning submission, and

[1] Grimm's "Correspondence," Part I., tom. iii., p. 48 (Longchamps, Paris; 1813).

all that had formerly produced great men and glorious actions for France. And this prejudice, where it was established, was so deeply rooted that one of the literary men does not hesitate to write [1] "The time is not far off when people will rejoice at losing the two or three men of genius who remain to France." About the same time, in 1760, the reception address to the French Academy was made the occasion of a violent diatribe against the new literary school by M. Le Franc de Pompignan; not many months later M. J. G. Le Franc de Pompignan, Bishop of Puy, in a pamphlet entitled, "Instruction Pastorale," rivalled his brother of the Academy in branding the author of the "Henriade," the author of "Emile," and the rest, as the source of the growing irreligion and anarchism.

Coming to later times, we find the Catholic De Bonald accusing Voltaire of being the author of the misfortunes of France and Europe by having caused the widespread hatred of things solemn and grave through his philosophic mockery; and De Maistre follows him in styling Voltaire an insolent blasphemer and the personal enemy of the Saviour of men. The appellation of the "Revolutionary Man," which St. Just, in 1794, gave to Rousseau, has more than once been

[1] Grimm's "Correspondence," Part I., tom. iii., p. 29 *et seq.*

repeated by later historians, and the "Contrat Social" has been equally frequently branded as the source of inspiration of all the extravagance which characterised the Jacobin Government, so provokingly misnamed the "Democratic Republic." Michelet supported the same view of the case when in his history he remarked that the work of the Revolution was done when Voltaire and Rousseau breathed their last.

It was on the occasion of the celebration of the centenary of Voltaire's death in 1787 that Victor Hugo, who might not unreasonably be styled the Voltaire of the nineteenth century French literature, said of the French philosophers of the eighteenth century: "Those powerful writers have disappeared; but they have left us their soul and spirit, the French Revolution. Yes, the Revolution is their soul. It is their ever-shining spiritual radiation. It comes from them; they are to be found everywhere in this blessed and superb cataclysm which has closed the past and opened up the future."

Amongst the later exponents of this view in France may be mentioned one of the most respectable names in history, that of M. Taine, who, in his "Ancien Régime," takes a rather exaggerated estimate of the influence of the literary and speculative activity of the eighteenth century, and who gives to books and doctrines the place which belongs more properly to dissolving institutions and a crumbling social and economic system. "The philosophy of the eighteenth century contained poison," remarks M. Taine, which affected the whole of France, and set it reeling like a drunken man, till the symptoms developed into convulsions; and he again compares it to a magazine of powder—piles of wood a long time accumulated—which in their conflagration involved the ruin of France.[1]

In England, as early as 1793, Burke had familiarised the minds of men with the cabal of literary and philosophic men in France under the Bourbon rule, who had formed "a regular plan for the destruction of the Christian religion, and who, intriguing with foreign princes and cultivating the alliance of the moneyed classes, hoped to inaugurate a new era in French history by force, if not by persuasion."[2] Lord Brougham, while controverting Mounier's views on the subject, emphasised the enormous influence of the writings of the literary men on the tone of French thought and action, and ridiculed those who "were prepared to believe, on seeing a battery erected against a town, and bearing its fire upon the walls for weeks, that

[1] "Ancien Régime," English Trans., pp. 327, 328.
[2] "Burke's Works," Payne's edition, vol. ii., p. 130 *et seq.*

the breach which was made had not been caused by bullets, but by an accidental earthquake."[1] But what if it had not been an accidental earthquake, but rather a kind of internal corruption and disorganisation among the besieged? Would that have been an irrational way of speaking?

The traditional way of speaking amongst the early historians of the Revolution in England has not been inaptly summarised by Lord Lytton in his "Parisians": "Had there been no Voltaire there would have been no Camille Desmoulins; had there been no Diderot there would have been no Marat."[2] This traditional view may be said to find unwarranted support in the statements made by Mr. John Morley, who says in his work on Rousseau: "It was his work more than that of any other one man that France arose out of the deadly decay which had laid hold of her whole social and political system, and found that irresistible energy which warded off dissolution within and partition from without."[3] To those acquainted with Mr. Morley's treatises on the French philosophers, it is a fact well known that such a statement hardly finds any confirmation in his writings; but, at the same time, statements like these are significant as showing a strong tendency,

[1] "Statesmen of the Reign of George III.," pp. 11, 12.
[2] Vol. ii., p. 183.   [3] "Rousseau," vol. i., p. 3.

hitherto prevalent among a large number of those conversant with the history of the epoch, to attribute the Revolution to the writings of the eighteenth century literary men.

This tendency may particularly be observed amongst those who write histories for school and college purposes, or popular expositions of the period concerned. We will only quote one instance among many. Mr. G. B. Adams, in his "Growth of the French Nation," remarks:[1] " Probably the most decisive of any single set of causes in leading to the Revolution was the intellectual, because it supplied arguments and guiding theories, and intense conviction, and, not the least important, sentimental motives. The philosophy of the eighteenth century, by carrying conviction with it, did more than all else to undermine the resistance of the classes who would be most naturally opposed to a Revolution." And a little later we have the following remark: " Voltaire proved the necessity, Rousseau furnished the motive force, for the Revolution." The same view appears to be advocated by Mr. J. H. Rose when he observes that the Revolution would have broken out as early as the death of Louis XV., owing to the influence of the philosophers and men of letters, had it not

[1] Macmillan & Co. : p. 268.

been put off by economic causes;[1] and likewise by Frederic Harrison in his essay on "What 1789 did."[2] Mr. Lilly's work on the subject reminds us somewhat of the diatribe of Burke against the French philosophers, as the potent authors of all the mischief, imaginable and real, of the succeeding epoch; and perhaps it is not altogether a regrettable circumstance that we have no historian in England of Taine's merits but with Taine's prepossessions.

Often have the philosophers of the Ancien Régime, in the style of Chateaubriand's invective against Napoleon, been termed the sophists of a new era of enlightenment, the corrupters of youth, the preachers of atheism, and the destroyers of morals—the cankers eating away the core of the nation's vitality in silence. Like the Jews and Christians in the first two centuries of our era, and not unlike the British Government in India from the standpoint of a few radical reformers, the philosophers were made responsible for all the evils that happened to characterise the period, and were made the scapegoats in whose blood were to be wiped off all the sins of the nation. And whereas the sophists have found an advocate in Goethe,

[1] "Revolutionary and Napoleonic Era."
[2] "Meaning of History," a collected edition of his essays, etc.

and the impartiality of philosophic criticism has recognised the limits of their responsibility; whereas the mere lapse of time has changed the judgment of history with reference to the Jews and the early Christian community; the philosophers will for a long time to come have to listen to the thrilling cry—" To the Lions!"—they will continue to be styled the authors of mischief, and their writings will be regarded by uncritical common sense as the source of the Revolutionary horrors. So long as the principles of the French Revolution continue to belong to the sphere of present-day politics, the philosophers of the pre-Revolutionary era will continue to be subjects of party vituperation and declamation.

It is against this view so generally held that the following essay is directed. We shall endeavour to ascertain how far facts can bear out the assertion that the writers of the Ancien Régime were responsible for the outbreak of the Revolution; how far history enables us to endorse the view that the occurrence of the Revolution and the virulence of its outbreak were influenced mainly by the French philosophers and their doctrines. The development of the Revolution may have brought into the foreground, for the time being, men who were staunch followers of the eighteenth century political and philosophical doctrines, and its spread throughout Europe may have been due to the ground being prepared for its reception by the writers of the Ancien Régime; these are facts with which we are not concerned for our present purposes. Our object rather is to show that these writers were not the potent authors of the Revolution; and that rather than themselves leading the French people to the Revolution, they were themselves led by the upper classes in France.

CHAPTER II

NO REPUBLICAN PARTY EXISTED IN FRANCE UNDER THE ANCIEN RÉGIME

To begin with, we entirely agree with M. Aulard in his judgment that, up to the time of the convocation of the States-General in 1789, there was not a single trace of any organised republican party in France.[1] The *Cahiers*, or the instructions given to the deputies to the States-General, which express the general wishes and aspirations of the whole nation, demonstratively prove to us that not only the nobles and the clergy, but likewise the vast majority of the nation, were staunchly monarchical in their sentiments. The only exception to this was found by the Abbé Maury in the case of the Duke of Orleans, whose personal aspiration was to substitute his own person on the throne for that of the King, and who, the Abbé said, denounced the King to the three Orders in his "Instructions to the Deputies." The only trace of the denunciation we find in the Instructions is an injunction to the

[1] "Histoire Politique de la Revolution Française," pp. 1, 2.

deputies "to conduct themselves according to what the public good may dictate rather than according to the regulations sent to them by the King, the reason being that the King had on no preceding occasion joined any regulations to the letters of convocation."

In short, up to 1789, no republican party could be found in France. Among the writers and philosophers of the Ancien Régime not a single man could have been designated as a republican. Montesquieu decisively praised the English monarchical system, and his "Esprit des Lois" is a standing protest against all attempts at finding out an ideal form of government. "An incomparable interpreter of facts," Montesquieu is always ready to penetrate into their *raison d'être;* he never stops to discuss their legitimacy. The very breadth of his intellect prevented him from impeaching the political *status quo*, by endowing him with a kind of optimism. With him every actually existing government is presumably good for that country merely because of the fact that it is the creation of historical circumstances and the product of a slow growth.

Voltaire's political ideal was that of a benevolent despotism, as is but too apparent to those familiar with his historical writings—a kind of government in which the ruler had unlimited authority and a real interest in the welfare of his subjects. Louis XIV., entering the hall of the Parliament with a riding whip in his hand, and pronouncing the words, "I am the State," was no despicable hero in his eyes. And it was this conception of the State that was in his mind when in 1753 he criticised incidentally, in his "Supplement to the Age of Louis XIV.," Montesquieu's position that "virtue is not the principle of a monarchy."

He observes: "I daresay I have understood by the despotism of Louis XIV. the ever-firm and sometimes too large use that he made of his legitimate power. If occasionally he caused the laws that he ought to have respected to yield to his power, posterity will condemn him; it is not for me to judge. But I doubt whether anybody can show to me any monarchy on earth in which the laws, distributive justice and the rights of man, have been less trampled under foot, and where greater things have been done for the public good than during the fifty-five years that Louis XIV. ruled by himself."[1] When Louis XVI. ascended the throne, and Turgot was called to the Ministry, Voltaire believed that a new era was beginning for France, when the old prejudices

[1] Collected edition of his works, Garnier Frères, 1883, vol. xv., p. 115.

would disappear, and reason would be freed from political restraints. Condorcet, whilst writing the life of his literary colleague, found himself compelled to defend Voltaire's preference for a monarchical form of government rather than his preference for republicanism. Voltaire's love for the people in general did not arise from any active democratic sentiment; it was rather a kind of pity such as an aristocrat might feel—a mixture of haughtiness and contempt. And such a tone of feeling would never for a moment have allowed him to condone the action of the people in trying and beheading their lawful sovereign.

If D'Argenson is found praising the republican form of government, it is only because he is inspired with the desire of seeing the Monarchy adopting for its own purposes the good attributes of a republic. If Helvetius had sometimes fulminated against kings, nowhere did he express a desire in his writings for the establishment of a republic in France. Like Rousseau, he praised the free but petty republics of the Greeks; like Montesquieu, he condemned all despotic states, and indiscriminately included all absolute monarchies under the condemnation. But he nowhere directly agitated in his writings the question whether a constitution which was so appropriate to the petty republics of Greece was suited to a large state like France.

So likewise Diderot's ideal of government did not much differ from that of his colleagues, and when he wished that the Society of Jesus which had worked so much mischief should be abolished, the best expedient he could think of was that of appealing to the Duc de Choiseul, the prime minister of the day. History has not hitherto given the slightest support to the conjecture that Diderot was the author of some dithyrambic, cannibalic songs known as the "Furieux de la Liberté," in which monarchical government is ridiculed and abused, and the belief in Providence raved at. On the other hand, the dedication to the "Father of the Family" lays down the ideal of a good monarch who governs for the good of his people.[1] He should recompense the men of merit, encourage hard-working subjects, come into closer and closer contact with them; and, above all, hunt out and bring to the front the men of genius who might be lying concealed or uncared for in the country.

The political ideal of the Encyclopædia, as Champion says, was a mixed form of government, consisting of monarchical, aristocratic, and democratic elements, suggested mainly by the writings

[1] Works Ed., 1798 Desray, Paris, vol. iv., p. 248 *et seq.*

of Montesquieu. All the most important political articles in which the institutions of the day were criticised assumed as the basis of their criticism a liberal monarch who had the good of his people at heart; if these defective institutions were reformed in time, a new era of prosperity would dawn for monarchical France. In one of the articles, for example, the note of warning was distinctly sounded against the growing centralisation of power; and if Turgot's plans of decentralisation had succeeded, they would have fulfilled all the aspirations of the Encyclopædists in that respect.

Representing the views of the leading French literary men, they wrote that the best present which the gods could give to men is that of a king who loves his people, and who is loved by them; who trusts in his neighbours, and has their confidence in return; and whose justice and humanity make foreign nations envy the happiness of living under his sway. They quoted with approval the sentiments of the author of "Telemachus on the Authority of Kings": "They have an absolute power to do good, but their hands are tied down if they endeavour to do mischief" So likewise, under the heading "Republic," we read in their work the remarks: "It is of the nature of a republic that it should have a small territory;

without that it cannot subsist. In a great republic there are too large fortunes, and consequently little moderation. The property is too temptingly large to be entrusted to a citizen; and every man feels that he can be happy, great, and glorious without his country." And a little further on we are told.: " It is certain that the tyranny of a prince does not bring his country nearer to ruin than the indifference for the commonwealth does with reference to a republic." One feels as if he were only reading a new edition of Montesquieu's "Spirit of the Laws," some passages of which are inspired by the teaching of the great apostle of liberty, the author of the " Contrat Social." If such were the views of many, and these the most advanced leaders of thought of the eighteenth century, one feels inclined to ask: Where, then, did the cabal against the existing Government of France thrive?

A few days after the death of Louis XV., we find Grimm writing in the following strain:[1] "Let the people who are often precipitate in their judgment, and more often exaggerated in their complaints, reproach him with the weakness of his latter years; a more equitable posterity will always admire in him the primary virtues of a great prince—clemency and bounty.... It will celebrate the religious humanity with which he condescended

[1] " Correspondence," Part II., tom. iii., p. 86.

to protect the unfortunate family of Calas against the injustice of one of his greatest tribunals and the superstition of a whole province. It will venture to say without fear and without adulation that a rule of nearly sixty years, in which no act of hatred or violence could be detected, must be placed in the rank of the happiest reigns."

To Rousseau, the advocate of the sovereignty of the people, the idea of a French Republic seems *ab initio* absurd. A state has a different form of government according to its size or extent. "If in different states," he remarks, "the number of supreme magistrates ought to be in inverse ratio to the number of citizens (that is to say, the more the state increases in extent, the more the number of governors should diminish), it follows that, in general, democratic government is suitable to small states, aristocratic to medium states, and monarchical to large states." Not only so, but the man who has been supposed to be the apostle of democracy remarks, in the course of his "Contrat Social," that democracy suffers from one fatal inconvenience that it is generally impossible to realise.[1] "If there were a nation of gods, there could be a democracy. A government so perfect does not suit men."

Throughout all his writings there appears a

---
[1] "Contrat Social," Book III., chap. v.

tendency, express or implied, to condemn revolution and rash changes of every kind. In the dedication to the "Discourse on the Origin of Inequality," he says: "People once accustomed to masters can no longer do without them; if they try to shake off the yoke, they alienate, so far, liberty from themselves; since mistaking a frightful licence for liberty, their revolutions only cause their chains to be more stringently riveted." His advice to the Poles in 1772, when they consulted him on the means of reforming their country, was "not to shake their machine too abruptly"; and Chateaubriand's surprise at the men of 1793 adopting as their teacher the works of Rousseau, "whereas there are no books which condemn them more," is but too well grounded. When Lally Tollendal said that Rousseau would have died of grief in the second month of the Revolution, and when Buzot thought that he would have perished on the scaffold with the Girondins, they both bore witness to the truth of the present contention.

D'Alembert, in his "Elements of Philosophy," refuses to say definitely which is the best form of government, and remarks: "The best republic is that which by the stability of laws and uniformity of government most nearly resembles a good monarchy, and the best monarchy one in which the supreme authority is not more arbitrary than in a republic."

Grimm, in his "Correspondence," speaking of the political philosophy of his times, says:[1] "Nothing is easier than to expound in fine writings, with a good deal of eloquence, all the advantages of liberty; but where does it exist; in what corner of the earth does it reside in the manner in which it is represented in books? That is the question to which no easy reply is possible. The phantom of despotism is not better known than the chimera of liberty."

Elsewhere in Grimm we find an anecdote too curious to be passed over without notice. An English officer in garrison at Gibraltar went one day on a tour to the Coast of Africa, and fell in with a citizen of one of the towns. "It is a pity," said this citizen of a despotic autocracy, "to see you obliged to live in that nest of yours where you are perched with your compatriots, and annoyed to death." The Englishman, getting curious, asked him the sort of life that he led under his Government. He paid nothing to the State, nobody ever meddled with him, and he was accountable to no one for what he did, if he abstained from robbery and murder. The

[1] "Correspondence," Part I., tom. iv., p. 355.

Englishman asked him to take him over the Governor's palace. "Oh, no! he is a vicious man who cuts off his subjects' heads like cabbages. I have nothing to do with him; it little matters to me whether he is good or bad." A man of talents who could thus compare the life of an African subject of a despotic state with the restrained life of a citizen of a European constitutional government, bored to death by a thousand petty formalities and legal impediments, much in favour of the former, could hardly be styled a republican. And yet at every step in the history of the Ancien Régime we meet with the assertion that the literary men of the times were active republicans.

The Abbé Reynal, the author of the History of the Indies, one of the philosophic group of the eighteenth century, who lived long enough to see the disastrous consequences towards which the Revolution was tending, was no more a republican than Voltaire or Rousseau, Turgot or Vergennes. When in his history he touches upon the question which was then agitating all minds, the question, viz., as to who were the persons who could save France from the impending ruin, he answers by pointing to the throne as the only instrument of salvation. The King alone could be the means of redressing all grievances, and of ensuring the greatness of the kingdom.

The same idea is found governing the minds of the statesmen of the Ancien Régime and of the Revolution. Turgot, than whom none represented better the spirit of the times—the spirit of benevolent despotism—and who might have been the enlightened minister of a virtuous sovereign, like Pombal in Portugal, or Florida Blanca in Spain, had for his one aim to make the throne the centre of all reforms in France. "Give me five years of despotism," he said, "and France will be free" He wished for and projected almost all the reforms which the Revolution afterwards effected for France; only had his projects been executed, they would have emanated from the throne, instead of emanating from the National Assembly.

Condorcet's grand proposal for a new system of public instruction would have proved of greater benefit to the nation under Louis XVI. than it did when, mutilated at the hands of Napoleon, it became a docile instrument of power and despotism. Throughout his short but eventful career, Mirabeau's central object was to strengthen the power of the Crown in order to make it the source of all reforms, and to oppose all attempts at weakening it, for fear of anarchy which might destroy the reforms along with the throne.

Even when we turn to men who were to organise the Republic in 1792, we find that the majority of them were monarchists in 1789. Lafayette, the darling hero of the American Revolution, was the patron of royalty; "to be a Washington under Louis XVI. was the dream of his life." Though he did much in the pursuit of his own ambition to weaken the power of the monarch whom he professed to honour, he would have discarded the idea of a republic in 1789 with contempt. Camille Desmoulins, the friend of Danton in 1792, compared Louis XVI. to Trajan in 1789. Not one of the many hundreds of deputies who were sent to Paris in 1790 to celebrate the first anniversary of the fall of the Bastille would have desired the establishment of a republic, though there were many amongst them who were to become prominent figures in the years which followed. Even Robespierre did not dream of a republic when he moved along in 1789 in the stately procession from Paris to Nôtre-Dame.

Thus the existence of a republican party in France in the pre-Revolutionary era may be said to be one of those bugbears with which history has made us so familiar. The people of Paris, supposed to be so deeply imbued with the spirit of republican and revolutionary agitation, cared more for their theatres and ordinary amusements than for political interests. In 1753, it might have been expected that the struggle of the Parliament with the King over the Bull Unigenitus would attract all the attention of a republican party, if any such existed in the country. It is observed, however, by a contemporary writer, that these events hardly lasted for twenty-four hours as the subject of public conversation at Paris, and that they never obtained a third of the attention that was paid to a revolution that had just then taken place in music by the arrival of Italian actors. The literary circles and coteries, of which there were so many in Paris and in France, which should have faithfully re-echoed the republican propagandism, if any such existed, concerned themselves more in speculating about the merits and demerits of a newly-elected member of the Academy than in discussing the political value of the Parliamentary Remonstrances that were now and again issuing from the press.

It was not the "Contrat Social" or "The Dijon Discourse," but the publication of a "Letter on Music," hardly known even to students of French literature, that almost secured for Rousseau the martyrdom of exile ; and the Pioneer of the Revolutionary drama, as he has frequently been styled, received more attention by the agitation of a question of art than he did by the publication of a political work, denounced by prejudice as "the gospel of anarchy." The fanaticism of the times exhibited itself in burning in effigy the author of this attack on French music, rather than in hailing with applause the preacher of uncompromising democracy.

The intellects of the French labourers and cultivators in the provinces were better suited to hail with delight any practical measures of relief, like the abolition of the Corvées in particular districts by Turgot, and to sing *Te Deums* for the benefits conferred by the King, than to understand and espouse the abstract notions of the "sovereignty of the people" and "the will of the nation." And the risings in Brittany, La Vendée, and the provinces in the south, which broke out during the progress of the Revolutionary epoch, corroborate the inference we have been endeavouring to establish, namely, that France was entirely a stranger to a republican party under the Ancien Régime.

We do not, therefore, exaggerate when we say that on the eve of the Revolution there was no republican party, not a single individual who would publicly have wished to see a republic established in the kingdom. Those who knew the

c

history of France were all familiar with the fact that the throne had identified itself with the cause of reform, "because the King had appeared to be the opponent of feudalism, of local tyrannies, the protector of the communities of the inhabitants against all aristocracies." The Monarchy had not only established an orderly government in France, but had enlarged her dominions and made her dreaded abroad. It had been the means of ensuring to her one language, uniform customs, and a quasi-uniform administration. It had spread a high form of civilisation through the country by constituting itself the patron of literature and the arts.[1] It had "fostered the sense of nationality."

All this was known and appreciated by the rich and the learned, who claimed to represent the French nation. When, therefore, in 1789 the King, echoing the wishes of the nation, had himself headed the movement of reform by calling together the States-General, the whole nation seemed to have rallied round him, with one hope of approaching felicity, and one sentiment of loyalty to the throne. And if the history of the year 1792, the year of the establishment of the Republic, is carefully studied, it will reveal the fact that the Republic was forced on an all-

[1] A. J. Grant, "French Monarchy," vol. ii., p. 273.

reluctant majority by a handful of men, and that on the day before it was actually proclaimed, the announcement would have been received with incredulity and ridicule by all who were outside the minority elect.

CHAPTER III

REPUBLICAN IDEAS UNDER THE ANCIEN RÉGIME

But though an organised republican party was in France under the Ancien Régime a fiction unverified by history, republican *ideas* were not unknown. The philosophers themselves, whom we have considered above as monarchists, betray in some places in their writings other ideas, phrases, maxims and suggestions, held consciously or unconsciously, and highly detrimental to the principles of the divine right of monarchy. Afraid of the abuses of regal authority, they were desirous of restraining this authority by the aid of laws. They analysed the conception of the royal power, with a view to regulating its exercise. They sought for the origin of this authority in reason, in history, in the consent of men, in the national will; and they all seemed to have combined to undermine the Catholic religion on which this authority was mainly based.

Montesquieu praised the republican form of government when he wrote that it was founded on virtue, whereas a monarchy was founded on honour. His "Spirit of the Laws" has not inaptly been called an exaggerated satire on the monarchy, by one who took no mean part in the early period of the Revolution[1] His "Lettres Persanes"[2] are not without their share of indirect fling at "the great magician monarch," who could make his people believe that he could cure them of all kinds of evils by touching them. In not a few of these letters did he sound a note of warning against the abuses of the *de facto* Government in France. In the 107th letter he writes· "Above all, my dear Rhedi, what I have before said is plain, that a prince who will be powerful must be careful that his subjects be well protected and prosperous; he must strive that they should not only be well supplied with the necessaries of life, but that they should have every superfluity of luxury." The philosophic standpoint that he adopted in judging of history and its data, particularly in his "Considerations on the Decay of the Romans," indirectly dealt the greatest blow to the theory of divine right.

Voltaire wrote in 1752 that a "republican is always more attached to his country than a subject to his, since he loves better what is

---

[1] Mounier.   [2] Lettre xxiv.

good for himself than what is good for his master." The article Democracy in the "Philosophic Dictionary" gives a positive preference to the republican form of government over all others, viewing the question as an abstract discussion. An enemy of all chimeras, of all dreamers, of all fanatics, he spent a whole life in attacking old-fashioned theories and prejudices and traditions; and his principal contribution towards the formation of a republican spirit in France was his attack upon the Christian religion, allied, as we have seen, so closely with the throne. The withering sarcasm which he brought to bear on the dogmatic part of Christianity was supplemented by a sceptical rationalism which refused to believe in a special revelation and a chosen people. And the tottering Church helped on the work of slow destruction by laying herself open to attack by incidents like those of Calas and La Barre. The patriarch of Ferney could claim to be the champion of suffering humanity by espousing the cause of persecuted Huguenots; and the State, by mixing itself up with an unpopular cause, shared in the general discredit into which the Church had fallen.

As for Rousseau, by his theory of the Social Compact, he traced all existing political authority to the sovereign people who had originally entered into a compact with each other to defend their persons and property; and he gave a right of insurrection to all whenever that compact was supposed to be broken. But whilst laying the foundation for the doctrine of the sovereignty of the people, he was at the same time preaching the omnipotence of the State, which had an absolute authority over each member of the body politic, his property and his actions. The State which represents the sovereignty of the people is all-powerful, and every individual who opposes the will of the majority, or the "general will," is to be forced to obey by the State. Thus the apostle of the new creed of "liberty, equality, fraternity," proved to be the advocate of the most autocratic absolutism that could have been imagined, and the annihilation of the individual for the benefit of the State—the main idea of the Social Compact theory—became the best commentary on republican delusions, if any such there were in France.

Writing later on, under the heading "Political Economy," in the Encyclopædia, Rousseau says: "There are three conditions of a legitimate government. The first is that the law should be the expression of the general will; wherever the law is the expression of the particular will of a single man, or of a few men, there is tyranny. Secondly, the general will will always be just, because the citizens will be brought up under conditions fitted to make them love justice. Hence the education of its citizens will be the second condition of a legitimate government. The third is to provide for the public needs." Were these conditions fulfilled by the French monarchy of his time? No, said Rousseau, and this tone of dissatisfaction underlies all his political writings. If we argue, however, on the lines of the earlier "Dijon Discourse," we are compelled to go further. If inequality in property and the consequent injustice is due to what we style civilisation, and the return to an imaginary state of nature—the golden age of the people living under the Social Compact—be advisable, then the modern States of Europe deserve to be overthrown by an all-powerful hand, and a revolution in the sphere of politics is absolutely essential. But age sobered down the denouncer of modern civilisation, and forced him to acknowledge historical development as a factor not to be altogether neglected.

The Encyclopædia, counting amongst its contributors all the representative writers and eminent men of the eighteenth century, from Montesquieu and Turgot to Condorcet and Morellet, counting among them, as Voltaire observed, officers of war, magistrates, physicians, geometers, and physicists, had for its broad aim the advancement of human happiness by means of knowledge. It therefore applied itself, amongst other things, to a critical investigation into the origin of society, the history of religions, and the government and all the branches of administration. In searching articles it exposed the shortcomings of the French Government, and traced the causes of the rise and fall of various forms of constitutions.

Moreover, the political theories of Rousseau were not entirely unknown to the Encyclopædia. Under the heading State might be found the following remarkable sentiments: " Two things contribute principally to maintain the State. The first is the engagement itself by which private individuals submit to the rule of the Sovereign ; the second is the establishment of a superior power, adequate to put down the recalcitrant by the fear of penalties which it can inflict on them. It is, then, the union of a number of human individuals voluntarily consenting to obey a superior power which gives rise to a state. Without this, a civil society is inconceivable." Certainly this is not far from the Social Compact, with its double-edged argumentation.

The writings of Diderot, D'Holbach, and other members of the Encyclopædic group, contributed further to swell the tide that was rising against the

Christian religion; and every blow that affected Christianity affected the Monarchy. The treatise of Helvetius on "L'Esprit," which Diderot happily termed the "preface to the 'Spirit of the Laws' of Montesquieu," had for its predominant object the destruction of prejudices in every direction, and it was in this respect a faithful exponent of the prevailing tone of thought amongst the classes to which it appealed.

Condorcet, writing in 1789, says: "The person of the King is sacred, because his authority is legitimate, and because he is the depositary of the forces of the citizens to make the laws respected. Thus in our monarchy the nation expresses the general will; the general will makes the law; the law gives rise to the King and to the executive power." Apparently an echo of the Social Compact theory. Sentiments to the same effect are expressed in different ways by Reynal, Mirabeau, Sieyès, Cerutti, and Mounier. The idea that the King is but a citizen, obeying the laws and causing them to be enforced, had been known and popularised for a long time before 1789, and is but one of the proofs that ideas of a republican type were familiar to the educated and upper classes of the Ancien Régime.

It is but too obvious, therefore, that the French literature of the eighteenth century teemed with doctrines prejudicial to the throne. The question before us is whether this literature was the original propagator of republican doctrines amongst the upper and learned classes in France; whether the philosophers of the Ancien Régime were mainly responsible for the rise of the spirit which ultimately overthrew the monarchy in 1792; or whether these philosophers sailed along a current of thought whose trend was determined by causes entirely independent and different. It is this latter view that we shall endeavour to establish—the view, namely, that the philosophers, instead of being the cause, and the main cause, were only the manifestation of the revolutionary spirit which was agitating the French political atmosphere; and far from leading that spirit, they were only led by it in turn.

CHAPTER IV

THE CONTINUITY OF EUROPEAN HISTORY

To those conversant with the general course of European history the remark is but commonplace that the principal tendency characteristic of the entire period extending from the Renaissance and Reformation down to the Revolution of 1789—a tendency which marks off likewise the work of the Revolution itself—is the emancipation of the individual from the trammels of tradition and authority. The main result of the Middle Ages for Europe had been to "impart a heavenly origin and a divine consecration"[1] to all human institutions; "all that existed was unassailable, not because it was good, but simply because it existed." The authority of men was substituted for that of reason; books were studied more closely than nature; and the opinions of the ancients received more attention than the phenomena of the universe around. This mental servitude was supplemented

[1] Sybel's "French Revolution," English translation by Perry, vol. ii., Book V., Chap. i.

by a physical and political servitude in the major part of the European Continent, a servitude which reached down to the humblest functions of the life of the individual citizen.

The Renaissance was the first revolt on the part of the human individual to shake off his servitude, a revolt of which the Reformation forms a continuation. It radically changed men's conceptions of life and nature, and freed them from the powers which controlled them in the Middle Ages. "The fundamental theme of the Middle Ages was the restoration and glorification of the 'Civitas Dei,' that kingdom of God on earth which rules the world and binds individuals. The fundamental theme of the Renaissance starts from the completely opposite key; it consists in the glorification of man, his greatness and his fame; in the worship of the individual, his genius, his power, his immeasurable natural freedom."[1] This was the chief result of the period, and governed the ablest actors of the drama, Machiavelli and Ficino, Peracelsus and Telesio, Raphæl and Michæl Angelo The absence of a central power in Italy was extremely helpful to the work of the Renaissance, and was a manifestation of the same spirit in

[1] Kuno Fischer, "Descartes and his School," English translation, p. 81.

the political sphere which inspired its intellectual and social sides.

The Reformation carried on this work of revolt against the Middle Ages, and attacked the old order of things on the religious side. The conscience of the human individual, and not the authority of the Church, was made the ultimate test for ascertaining the validity of religious truths; and though at first this was veiled under the ostensible object of an appeal to the Bible itself as against the traditional authority of the Roman Catholic Hierarchy, it revealed its individualistic tendencies with the lapse of time when it became clear that the interpretation of Biblical texts must in turn depend upon the intellectual insight of the interpreter.

And if the individual was thus rendered the central object concerned in a matter like religion, how much more necessary and natural it became that he should be made the test and criterion for all minor objects and purposes of life—whether for the purposes of political institutions like the State, or for those of his social and material interests. Galileo and Copernicus had already made the planetary system dependent on the sun, and confounded the traditional astronomical theories supported by the

Church. This critical attitude passed gradually from religion to politics, from the arts to the sciences, from legislation to industry.

In politics this tendency showed itself in the slowly proceeding disintegration of the unity of Europe, which had hitherto found expression in the shape of a Holy Roman Empire. The Mediæval Unity of the Church and State which had started into life, theoretically and practically, with the Empire of Charlemagne in 800, now gave way to a state of affairs in which decentralisation was the ruling factor, and the idea of nationality the germinating fruit. The various nations of Europe now for the first time began to form themselves into national units independent of any foreign influence.

From politics this spirit of individualism or humanism passed on to learning and the intellectual interests. The Renaissance had already produced men who turned their attention from the investigation of statements made by old writers to the investigation of natural phenomena. This work was continued during the Reformation period, and found the best help in Bacon. The invention of the art of printing led to the diffusion of learning and to the freedom of thought from traditional influences. The two Bacons, Giordano Bruno, Vannini,

Campanella, and the host of others who preceded Descartes, were the first symptoms of a storm which broke forth in Descartes himself. The philosophy of Descartes is the protest of the individual mind against the authority of the past represented by the scholastics, as the preaching of Luther was the protest of the conscience against the authority of the Church. And though for a time the individualistic traits of the philosophy of Descartes were absorbed and transformed in the universalism of Spinoza, they again reappeared in the Leibnizian monads and the Critiques of Kant.

And it is remarkable, as showing the continuity of all history, that the last phase of the Renaissance period, which found a reflection in the thoroughgoing scepticism of Montaigne and Charron, was the starting-point for the speculative activity of Bacon and Descartes. It was this same tendency to individualism that led to the gradual displacement of the Latin language in Europe by the mother tongues of the particular nations. The study of the sciences became more popular, and the growth of national sentiment was fostered. The freedom of thought from all external shackles was attended in France by the outburst of literary activity under Louis XIV. Bossuet, Fenelon, Molière, Corneille,

Racine, all in turn contributed towards raising the dignity of man, and inculcated a loftier view of his significance in the economy of the universe.

The rise of the industrial movement, as Comte terms it, by the gradual disappearance of slavery into serfdom, till serfdom itself was thinned away into freedom of the individual, was also a manifestation of the same tendency; and the substitution of the industrial for the military life in modern Europe spelt the revival of domestic life. The human family, whose interests had hitherto been entirely subordinated to the State on the one hand, and the Church on the other, now began to breathe again in a polity where its influence was recognised and allowed for. It spelt also the abolition of the Caste system, and set up against the principle of primogeniture and the authority of sacred traditions and birth, the principle of wealth acquired by industry. Inheritance of occupation yielded to the desire for improvement on the part of the individual; and gradually the emancipated classes asserted their influence in the sphere of government.

Such was the nature of the grand movement in the history of Europe which was inaugurated by the Renaissance, and carried on by the Reformation. The eighteenth century in Europe saw the further extension of the movement, till it was consummated, as it were, in the French Revolution. It was with no flinching hand that the Ancien Régime in France carried on the work of freeing the individual from all restraints that was delegated to it by the preceding ages; and it was just this work that the eighteenth century writers in France carried through to the end, knowingly or unknowingly. If there is any characteristic that distinguishes the whole of the eighteenth century literature in that country more saliently than any other, it is this same spirit of revolt against the past—the assertion of the rights of the individual, and the centralisation of all social, political, intellectual, and artistic interests in him as the pivot and turning axis. A cursory examination of French literary activity under the Ancien Régime will confirm this view.

CHAPTER V

THE PHILOSOPHERS AN EVIDENCE OF THIS CONTINUITY—INDIVIDUALISM

THE student of French literature in the pre-Revolutionary era will find it hardly a difficult task to trace the individualistic tendency of thought in all branches of learning and intellectual activity. Not that anti-individualistic strata of thought are absolutely absent in the literature of the period; sweeping generalisations of this kind are out of place in the sphere of social dynamics. What we will endeavour to emphasise in this and the following chapter is the circumstance that the tone of thought is predominantly individualistic, and where it is not directly so, it is so by implication and inference.

The writing of history was transformed into a peculiar art aiming at practical utility. History should not be a mere relation of facts, of kings, of battles, of treaties; such was the trend of thought of the eighteenth century writers.[1] It should rather be a relation of men, actions, and manners. A

[1] Grimm's "Correspondence," tom. i., Part I., p. 176 *et seq.*

fact is interesting only inasmuch as it illustrates character; a king does not merit the attention of the historian unless he is a hero **and** a *man*. Without these essential qualities the place of kings and of facts is not in history; we must relegate them to annals and useless almanacs, to serve as marks of chronology. Everything, therefore, that did not have a more or less practical bearing was to be excluded from history, and the scientific conception of history which was slowly dawning on the minds of men was to give place to the practical purpose of pointing a moral or adorning a tale—to a sort of memoir writing or biography for edifying the minds of men.

Nor was such a method of writing history without its practical illustration in the eighteenth century. Voltaire's History of Charles XII. and Reynal's History of the Indies may be called the classics of this new method. Even the obscure historians of the time, like the Abbé Velly, professed to follow it in their prefatorial remarks, even though they quietly laid it aside in the body of their works. And when history was reduced to the level of memoirs, it was but natural that memoirs should flourish and multiply to an indefinite extent. The eighteenth century memoirs are characterised more by their gossip about individuals than by their insight into the deeper currents of life, thus indicating the taste of the times, which was centred more in the individual than in the State or society.

The practical character, moreover, of history and historical compositions which the eighteenth century developed was shown in a different way in the range of topics dealt with by the histories of the times. Voltaire's "Age of Louis XIV." is not merely a chronological record of the events of that age, not merely a description of the wars and political intrigues, but includes within its scope a history of literary activity, a history of commercial development, a history of the progress made by the sciences and arts, a history of finance and financial experiments. We might even say that he subordinates all political events purely so-called to the history of civic development. And as if this were not enough, he writes a few years later a history of the "Morals, Manners, and Character of Nations." The importance given to these phases of national development is not confined to Voltaire, but operates on all the historical works that were produced in the Voltairian era. Mably, in his preface to his History of France, regrets that historians "should have neglected the origin of laws and customs in favour of sieges and battles." Ducos, in his introduction to the "History of Louis XIV. and XV.," remarks: "If the history that I am writing is neither political, nor military, nor economic, in the sense that I attach to these words, what is it, then, that I propose to write? It is the history of men and manners." The general enlargement of the scope of history indicates the importance attached to its study as a useful teacher of practical lessons to individuals and nations. All these topics were included within history, not because they afforded scope for scientific generalisation, but because they helped men to make themselves happier, and enabled them to keep in harmony with their surroundings.

If we turn to philosophy, the same individualism stares us in the face. The philosophy of Condillac and La Mettrie may be said to be the logical extension of Lockian modes of thinking in a one-sided direction, suggested by the provisional scepticism of Descartes. The individual was the starting-point; and the ultimate object of philosophy was taken to be the explanation of knowledge as the product of the sensations and feelings of the individual. Simple sensations and feelings were alone sufficient to develop into the complex synthesis which we term knowledge; and no unity or principle higher than the individual mind was necessary for the explanation of the universe and its constituents. The metaphysical speculations of the Cartesian school were relegated to the lumber-room of curious antiquities, much in the fashion of Hume; and the individual was made the central object of creation for whom the universe substituted, and whose needs it was made to serve. Abstract speculations about the nature of the soul gave place to physiology and physical experiments for ascertaining the reciprocal phenomenal relations of the mind to the body; and the question of metempsychosis was exchanged for the question whether animals had a soul or were automata. The historical treatment of the various philosophical systems had demonstrated the inutility of all such aerial speculations, and the philosophers now occupied themselves in devoting a closer attention to the natural sciences. The ontological arguments for the existence of God gave place to the historical argument which traced the belief in a Deity amongst barbarians, and its growth and development amongst all nations. The distinction between innate and acquired ideas in morals and metaphysics was transformed and annihilated in the attempt at treating morals and metaphysics as branches of experimental philosophy. The occasionalism of Malebranche was succeeded by a crude materialism, dogmatic in its tone and polemical in its essence.

Such was the philosophy of the eighteenth century leaders of thought which affected the whole tone of society, but which, at the same time, owed its rise to the society itself. The one remarkable thing about it was, that in spite of its materialistic attitude, it should have retained in full its faith in the destinies and progress of the human individual. The logical outcome of a consistent materialistic philosophy is to reduce man to a machine, and to sink into the despair of scepticism; but the eighteenth century writers were too obviously inspired with the ideas of progress and material and moral welfare to yield to the demands of speculative doctrines.

The drama was to be submitted, no less, to the principles of individualism and utility. M. Marmontel, in his "Poétique Française," a kind of eighteenth century French "L'Art Poétique," remarks: "If there is anything touching in the world of a drama, it is the spectacle of a man rendered guilty and miserable in spite of himself. But I would return incessantly to moral utility, with which the poet as a good man ought never to dispense." So likewise, while criticising an obscure play by Madame de Grafigny, Reynal remarked: "There is no man of genius in France who would not be glad to be the author of this play; it is the triumph of virtue, the temple of manners, the school of sentiment the purest and most simple, the best calculated to fix the attention of good persons." And the *good persons* of the critique meant only the most prominent portion of the theatrical audience, consisting of the upper classes of France, and more particularly those who resided in Paris. Thus the applause of the Parisian bourgeoisie and nobility became the standard for judging the worth of a theatrical composition, and their ideals the guide for dramatic authors.

To no branch of the French literature of the eighteenth century does Brunetière's reproach apply with greater truth than to dramatic writings—the French drama in that period was indeed the most effective illustration of the denationalisation and "deformation of the classic ideal." In comedy the successors of Molière contented themselves with merely describing what they had observed in actual life, with a little wit artistically introduced to excite laughter and please the requirements of the audience. The humour of the "Femmes Savantes" was replaced by the obscene wit and degenerated plays of Piron and Gresset. The tragedies of Corneille and Racine were forgotten in the mechanical versification and stage orations of the plays of Voltaire and Crebillon. Every part of the play, its whole structure, its tone, its divisions, its characters, and its dialogues, should be calculated to please the audience; and whatever the play may be, it should aim at the inculcation of a moral precept. This is the tenor of a long essay by Diderot on " Dramatic Poetry." If such be the rules for the composition of dramatic pieces, and such the ideal of its authors, there can be no wonder that the classical models of French drama should have been degraded into a mere caricature of their former selves. Poetry and drama cannot be made to submit to any standards of utility, and if they do, they cannot retain any more their proper nature and value.

If from the drama we turn to the eighteenth century idea of romance, the same phenomenon will meet us again. The Chevalier de Jaucourt tells us, in an interesting article in the Encyclopædia, that the finest romance in the world is " Telemachus." Tracing the history of romance, he remarks that the greater part of such compositions in his time were productions devoid of imagination, which spoiled the taste and disgusted the readers. How could they then be restored to their proper dignity? By rendering them *useful*. They could place before the mind examples of constancy, virtue, tenderness; their authors could depict their own best feelings in their works, and could place virtue, not in the skies and out of the reach of man, but on the earth, as being within the reach of human endeavour, the prize of a victory over enemies. The "Nouvelle Héloise," the Chevalier tells us, is the type of such a work, and proceeds upon the same lines as "Telemachus." So likewise Voltaire remarks that fiction which does not teach a truth or preach a moral is worth nothing, and is a dream and falsehood. But the composition of romances and novels plays a very unimportant part in the eighteenth century literature; nor was it to be expected that a generation of writers whose activities were mainly absorbed in the advancement of science in all its branches should find time to devote to light literature.

The multiplication of writings on commercial topics, and the large number of commercial works every year translated from foreign languages into French, is another illustration of the individualistic tendencies of the times. Political economy now gradually came to be looked upon as a science, whose laws could be framed into rules for the practical guidance of statesmen; and the wealth of nations came to be regarded as dependent upon laws whose operation might be directed by human endeavours into desired channels. But the wealth of nations was only, for the eighteenth century writers, the wealth of the aggregate of citizens who made up the nation; and the *physiocrats* who began to come into prominence endeavoured to apply these principles to the cultivation of land, on which, according to them, the prosperity of the nation ultimately rested. Thus political economy in the eighteenth century contributed in its own way to bring the interests of the individual to the foreground.

Nowhere, however, does this individualistic philosophy, with its revolt against the past, come into greater prominence than in the movement of the Encyclopædia. Aiming at the advancement of human happiness through the spread of knowledge, it devoted its main attention to the mechanical arts, as they were styled, in contrast with the so-called liberal arts. Anatomy, physiology, mechanics, agriculture and agricultural questions, chemistry, medicine, and all those other sciences and arts which contributed either directly or indirectly to the happiness of mankind, received the largest space, and were treated with ample minuteness, while the liberal arts were comparatively neglected.

If we turn over the pages of the now antiquated volumes, we will find ample illustrations of what we have been urging. Under the heading "Academy," for instance, in the first volume, only a few lines are devoted to the history of the French Academy, enlisting as it did in its membership the best talents in the nation, whereas two or three pages are assigned to the Academy of the Sciences, and to the Academy of Belle Lettres and Inscriptions. Abstract questions of metaphysics are subordinated to the practical questions of politics, political economy, sanitation, and what we now term natural history (botany and zoology). Thus the question of the equilibrium of bodies and the impenetrability of matter received greater consideration than the question of the immortality of the soul and incarnation.

Through each and every one of these volumes there breathes one spirit, one thought, one aspiration, to help on the work of scientific discovery and progress, so that the individual may be happier and better than he at present is. And along with this aspiration was inextricably involved another—that the methods of the past be abandoned, that the chains and fetters of the past be rent asunder, that the traditions of the past be crushed and rooted out. The spirit of Helvetius, when he remarked,[1] "It is by enfeebling the stupid veneration of people for laws and ancient usages that they will enable sovereigns to purge the earth of all

[1] "L'Esprit," Discourse II., chap. xvii.

the evils that desolate it," was the spirit which guided the Encyclopædic writers in their laborious and admirable work. It was not unknowingly that Voltaire made the senator Pococurante observe:[1] "I frequently asked learned men if they were not annoyed as much as myself at the incessant and repeated reading of Homer's 'Iliad'; all sincere men acknowledged to me that the book fell from their hands, but that it was necessary to have it in their libraries as a monument of antiquity, like those rusty medals which could not be exchanged." It was a significant commentary on the indiscriminating revolt against the past of the eighteenth century writers.

Whether this commentary be well or ill deserved, the revolt against the past is the keynote of the Encyclopædia, and is sounded most distinctly even in the Preliminary Dissertation. The respect for ancient things, for old authors, for former theories, must be abandoned, and a minute investigation of the facts concerning each particular science should alone occupy the attention of men. We hear the Renaissance note once again in this dissertation of D'Alembert· "The poetry of the Middle Ages was reduced to a puerile mechanism; the profound examination of Nature and the great

[1] "Candide," chap. xxv.

study of man were replaced by a thousand frivolous questions on abstract beings and metaphysics." " Let them add to this disorder the state of slavery into which the whole of Europe was plunged, the ravages of superstition that was bred of ignorance, and which was reproduced by it in its turn; and we shall see that nothing was wanting to complete the obstacles which prevented the return of reason and taste." The first step in the direction of liberation was taken by the Renaissance movement, in whose wake the Encyclopædia was proud to follow.

The note of warfare against the past breathes through all the writings of the Patriarch of Ferney. It expressed itself in an unreasoning hatred of the Middle Ages. The Middle Ages in Voltaire's works appear the potent source of human misery; they were really an age of darkness for him, when all social, intellectual, and religious activities of men suffered an eclipse, and were crushed out of all life. It was the same hatred of the past which made him deprecate and depreciate the value of the classical languages and literature which, according to him, crippled native originality and the development of national genius. And cannot this same hatred of the past among the eighteenth century writers in general be made to account for the fondness with which they clung to abstract theories about the natural rights of man, and which made them neglect the influence of institutions on human beings?

There is one more characteristic of the eighteenth century writings which illustrates in its own way the general movement in history which we have been emphasising. Whether we turn over the glowing pages of the Encyclopædia or consult the writings of Diderot, La Mettrie, and Rousseau, we find everywhere a firm faith in the possibilities lying before the human individual, a belief in the growth and development of moral and material prosperity for the world, bringing with it as a necessary consequence increased felicity for mankind; and Condorcet, hunted from place to place by the Jacobin Government, in constant and immediate dread of the guillotine, a few hours before his death, wrote the finishing sentences of his famous treatise expressing his staunch belief in the ever-increasing conquests of the human mind over nature and the obstructions of nature. At a moment when the shadows of the coming darkness were already closing around him, he was composing the last will and testament, as it were, of the eighteenth century writers, a race of men who expired in him.

But progress for the human race and general happiness were not possible unless the individuals composing the race participated in them. It was therefore the spirit of individualism that triumphed in the triumph of these ideas, and contributed its share towards the work of revolt against the past. The extensive progress made in all directions by the human intellect since the Middle Ages was due to the belief that such progress was possible; and it was just the absence of this belief, or rather its positive suppression, that accounts for the general inactivity in the period which saw the triumph of the schoolmen, and which has been deservedly called the Dark Ages. Such a characteristic as this, therefore, amongst the literary men in the Ancien Régime shows its essential harmony with the preceding ages.

CHAPTER VI

INDIVIDUALISM IN ETHICS AND POLITICS

SUCH was, then, the nature of the great individualistic reaction whose movements in the eighteenth century we have just been tracing. It remains to see (1) what theory of morals, and (2) what theory of politics would be in harmony with, and follow necessarily from, such data.

As regards morals, a philosophy that bases itself on the individual, and makes him the starting-point in the discussion of epistemological problems, can only arrive at individualistic hedonism in ethics. The exclusion of any principle higher than sense perception from the sphere of knowledge necessitates the exclusion of all springs of action higher than the sensuous from the sphere of morals. Accordingly, we find La Mettrie, with whom materialism had been carried out to its logical consequences, laying down that man's happiness rests upon the feeling of pleasure. Even the highest intellectual delights are in substance bodily pleasure. Virtue in an absolute sense is a delusion; a thing can be called good or bad only in relation to society. Virtue and merit are inventions made by society to induce men to do good to the commonwealth. The good, accordingly, is that in which public interests outweigh private interests; the bad, that in which private interests break through and injure public interests. Society, however, is nothing more than an aggregate of individuals; hence virtue ultimately resolves itself into procuring pleasures in the largest number to the greatest part of this aggregate. Benevolence, sympathy, pity, love, awe, reverence, self-abnegation, and all the best springs of conduct in men, must be explained away as derivative formations of self-love.

Such is the general tenour of La Mettrie's ethics, and such likewise that of all the leading men of the Ancien Régime. Diderot's essay on "Merit and Virtue" is only a re-edition of La Mettrie's work treated from the broader standpoint; but the "sum of pleasures" is still there, the supreme authority ranging the highest motives under its sway in accordance with their capacity of procuring happiness for the individual. Holbach, Grimm, and the whole Encyclopædic group were consistent followers of the ethics of La Mettrie, and showed their earnestness in the zeal with which they worked at the progress of the various sciences, and their more systematic application to the happiness of the individual.

This system of ethics was not, however, peculiar to the eighteenth century; it was only the development of ideas that had long ago been popularised by the essays of Montaigne and the philosophy of Bayle. And the scepticism of Montaigne, breathing through every chapter of his essays, and making merry at the expense of the loftiest instincts and feelings of man, was based on the idea that self-love is the ultimate spring of all action. There is nothing surprising in this: on the contrary, it is a circumstance which we would have been led, *à priori*, to anticipate from the nature of the data on which we have been working. If the eighteenth century literary and philosophical movement was a continuation of that which was first started by the Renaissance, the germs of such developed theories must necessarily have been present, obvious or concealed, in the Renaissance times; and Montaigne, who closes, as we observed, the Renaissance, was the natural precursor of La Mettrie and Holbach.

An ethical theory, based on such principles of selfishness, is best reflected in the practical lives of its literary exponents; and nowhere does this selfishness in theory display itself in practice in so brilliant colours than in the leader of the eighteenth century philosophers—Voltaire. The speculations of Holbach and Helvetius transformed themselves into practice when the man who wrote violent diatribes against the Duke of Orleans with the same hand signed humble petitions for his favour; when the man who, on the death of Madame du Châtelet, spoke of burying himself in monastic seclusion, a few days afterwards summoned a widowed niece to his side to help him in his dramatic compositions and performances. The scepticism of the times was best reflected in the man who accepted a pension from the King of Prussia, and when a quarrel ensued, called him "a monstrous pile of incongruities" and a "misanthropic brute."

Turning now to the question: What theory of politics would naturally result from such a movement? we might confidently expect that the same individualism would furnish the basis of political speculation in the eighteenth century. Society will be only an aggregate of individuals, and the ultimate *raison d'être* of political institutions will be the securing of pleasures or happiness to that aggregate. And if society is ultimately the number of individuals who constitute it, it can only have come into being by the voluntary consent of those individuals. The State then will be the result of a fortuitous concurrence of circumstances, and its existence due to a number of persons having thought that they could live better in that fashion than without it. Forms of government, in that case, are dependent on the ultimate consent of men for whose sake they exist, and to whom they owe their existence. Whenever, therefore, the expected happiness is not secured to the individuals by a particular form of government, it is natural and necessary that they should try to overthrow it and set up another. In all its acts, the government must consult the happiness of its subjects, and that alone.

Such is the theory of politics which we would naturally expect from the presuppositions of the eighteenth century philosophy, and such actually is the way in which the eighteenth century French writers express themselves. That government is a product of voluntary efforts on the part of individuals seems to be implied in one of the "Persian Letters":[2] "Would a prince desire that I should be his subject, when I reap none of the advantages of subjection?" Government is a kind of garment which the majority of individuals constituting it may put on and off according to his fancy. And though the historical conservatism of Montesquieu would

[1] Letter lxxvi.

never have permitted him to say such a thing in so many words, it was a conclusion which necessarily resulted from a mechanical view of society such as the eighteenth century held.

Holbach, in the "System of Nature," argues on the same basis: "As government," he says, "only derives its power from society, and is established only for its good, it is evident that society may revoke this power when its interests demand, may change the form of government, extend or limit the power entrusted to its leaders, over whom it retains a supreme authority by the immutable law of nature that subordinates the part to the whole."[1] And again: "By a covenant either expressed or implied, sovereigns engage themselves to watch over the maintenance, to occupy themselves with the welfare, of society; it is only upon these conditions that society consents to obey them." If by society we understand what the author of the "System of Nature" understood—viz., the aggregate of individuals constituting the society—we can see how these views on government were a natural corollary from the first principles of their political philosophy.

The *state of nature*, an imaginary condition of society in which each man individually was supposed to live apart and out of all relations to

[1] Chap. ix.

other men, which had led Hobbes to justify an absolute monarchy, led Montesquieu to his own theories in the "Esprit des Lois." And Voltaire, criticising Montesquieu, argues on the same individualistic basis. His *individual* is neither at absolute warfare with others, nor is he absolutely a peaceful creature.[1] "We have only to consider," he says, "the children of our rustics. The most cowardly flies before the most wicked; the feeblest is beaten by the strongest. If a little blood flows, he weeps and cries; the tears and complaints make a sudden impression on his comrade. He stops, as if a Superior Power had detained his hand; he is moved, affected, and embraces the enemy whom he wounded. Next morning, if there are nuts to quarrel over, they will fight again; they are already men; they will do the same later on with their wives and brothers." Arguing on this basis, Voltaire elsewhere remarks: "There has never been a perfect government, because men have passions; and if they had no passions, there would have been no government. The most tolerable of all is undoubtedly the republican, because it is that which brings men nearest to equality. Every father of a family ought to be the master in his house, but not in that of his neighbour. *A society being composed of several houses and several plots of land*

[1] Works, vol. xxx., p. 408.

attached to them, it is absurd that a single man should be the master of these houses and plots; and it is natural that each master should have an effective voice in the well-being of the society."[1]

We have already seen how Rousseau argued on his State of Nature to a government in which the sovereignty of the people would express itself in the will of the majority, and how the nation, assembled in its primary assembly, could make and unmake the executive authority according to their pleasure. Although the same presuppositions which led Rousseau to announce the sovereignty of the people made him announce the sovereignty of the State, with the annihilation of the individual for State purposes and his complete absorption into the State, yet the latter was left in the background, and the fact that the citizen as such had a millionth part of the total vote in making or unmaking his sovereign was dragged to the front and popularised.

There is one more feature of political importance that might be naturally expected to flow from individualism. The policy of the State in relation to religion must be a comprehensive toleration. If the individual and his happiness was the main concern of government, it was necessary that the State should not interfere with the particular

[1] Works, vol. xxiv., p. 425, "Idées Républicaines."

religious views which its members may profess, and all would come under its protection, whatever their faith or creed. There is not a single one of the eighteenth century writers in France who did not at one time or other write on *Toleration*, and show their hatred of religious fanaticism which took delight in persecution. The voice from Ferney which denounced to Europe the fanaticism of the Church in the persecution of Calas and La Barre re-echoed the sentiments of the whole literary circle of the times. The long and able article on Toleration in the Encyclopædia demonstrated the general interest in the question; it was a subject on which the eighteenth century writers never tired of descanting in a thousand forms and in a thousand places. It was a state of mind for which the eighteenth century people, and particularly the French people, were long prepared by the sectional quarrels between the Jesuits and Jansenists, the Calvinists and the Papists.

Thus we may say, without fear of contradiction, that the republican ideas and sentiments which may be found in the eighteenth century philosophers and literary men formed part of a general movement which began at the Renaissance, and which did not end till the Revolution completed the old era and marked the commencement of a new one. A theory which makes out society to be a mechanical agglomeration of individual units, and explains it as a mere arrangement between human individuals, takes away its *raison d'être*, and accustoms men to look upon law and government as fortuitous products, which can be destroyed and constructed according to the fancy of their moment. It is a sort of nominalism in politics: the individual is the real, the State a mere figment of the mind. It was the outcome of the Renaissance movement, and as the heirs to that movement, the eighteenth century writers necessarily gave expression to it. Where, then, lies the point of the remark that the eighteenth century philosophers in France were the authors of the republican propagandism which brought about the French Revolution itself? Literature has always been said to express the spirit of the times, to reflect the thoughts and action of a nation in the best and purest form; and this remark can never be more appropriately applied than to the eighteenth century literature in France under the Bourbons.]

CHAPTER VII

REVOLUTIONARY AGITATION A PECULIAR TRAIT OF FRENCH HISTORY IN GENERAL

THE eighteenth century French society, as it existed under the Bourbon rule, may, for our purposes, be roughly divided into two parts. To one of these parts belonged the King and his family, the nobility and the clergy, and the rich bourgeois, who had either by their learning or their wealth constituted themselves into a privileged class; in the other may be reckoned the vast majority of the nation: the one rich, the other poor; the one learned, the other ignorant and incapable of understanding the philosophical propaganda of the times. When we say, therefore, that the French writers of the Ancien Régime only interpreted the sentiments and intellectual tone of French society, the remark more specially applies to the former—the upper, the wealthy, and educated classes in France. It was their sentiments and life that was faithfully mirrored in literature rather than those of the *roturiers* and the poorer classes.

The Parlements of France represented the wealthy and educated classes in the country from early times, and those who are familiar with the early history of these bodies, and know how, from being merely judicial courts, they gradually assigned to themselves the right of interfering in the political administration of the country, need not be told how they fought against the royal prerogatives for a long time along with the nobility. The repressive measures of Richelieu, and the stern and almost absolute rule of Louis XIV., reduced the Parlements to their original status; but after the death of Louis XIV. they again asserted themselves as a power to be reckoned with by the royal dignitary; and the history of the struggle between Louis XV. and his Parlements amply illustrates the republican, or, at any rate, anti-monarchical sentiments of the educated classes in France. As early as 1726 we find it laid down in the consultations of the lawyers of the Parlement that "laws are really conventions made between those who govern and those who are governed." And again, in the Remonstrances of 1753, we find it stated by one of the sovereign courts, that "if subjects owe obedience to kings, the kings on their side owe obedience to the laws," and that "the nation stands above all kings as the Church stands above the Pope."

The men of letters in France as far back as the times of Richelieu wrote pamphlets and books, in which they asked in the name of reason, history, and justice what was the sanction for the absolutism of the royal power. The doctrine of the sovereignty of the people was clearly developed by a number of authors, amongst whom may be mentioned La Boëtie, Hotman, and Hubert Languet.[1] They announced that the King was only a servant of the nation, and that if he abused the authority of which he was the depositary, he could be deposed as a suspected traitor.

Hotman, in his celebrated "Franco Gallia," traces the elective nature of the Crown in history, and observes that the nation, having the power to elect kings, could remove them when they were no longer worthy of the office.[2] In Languet's work, or what is thought to be his work—*Vindiciæ contra Tyrannos*—we already find the "Contrat Social," a compact between the King and the people, and between God and the King, the King and the people both promising to be

[1] See M. Hanotaux, "Hist. de Card. de Richelieu," tom. i., p. 503.

[2] See "Souveraineté du Peuple," by Eichthal, p. 39.

faithful to God, and promising independently amongst themselves. From this double promise we have all sorts of consequences drawn by the author—armed resistance in case of violation and tyrannicide against the usurper. In the times of Louis XIV. books printed under the royal sanction speak of the mutual compact between kings and subjects. A treatise on the "Rights of the Queen to the different States of the Spanish Monarchy," published under the authority of the King, remarks "That the fundamental law of the State forms a reciprocal connection between the prince and his descendants on the one hand, and the subjects and their descendants on the other, by a species of contract which binds the sovereign to rule and the people to obey, a solemn engagement by which both parties agree to help each other." More than once, as we learn from Saint Simon, during the years succeeding the death of Louis XIV., the ominous word "Revolution" was heard during the discussions amongst the upper classes on political subjects.

Thus it may be said that before the outbreak of the Seven Years' War France had been for a long time familiar with republican views, and that the nobility and the educated classes had been accustomed to argue about the prerogatives of the King, and their origin and extent. But before the Seven Years' War the eighteenth century philosophers had not entered the field. The "Esprit des Lois" of Montesquieu appeared in 1748. The first volumes of the Encyclopædia were not published till 1751: the Voltairian era had not yet properly commenced, and if Voltaire had already appeared before the public, it was more as a dramatist than as a philosopher. Reynal had not yet come into public notice; and Rousseau was only known, if at all, as the author of the "Dijon Discourse." The spirit of discontent and criticism had been, in fact, firmly rooted in the upper classes and educated bourgeois of the Ancien Régime long before the eighteenth century philosophers had given their doctrines to the French public.

It was in 1713 that one P. Daniel published a History of France in three volumes, in which, with the artless air of a man who sought only to know the truth, he stated that the majority of French kings belonging to the first race were bastards, that several of the second race, and some even of the third, were equally the offspring of adultery; that this circumstance had not excluded them from the throne, and that they were never looked upon as having the slightest demerit in them which might disqualify them for the royal dignity. Never did a work create such interest as this for a short time. The nobility rushed for it; ladies of the highest rank fell in love with it; it was praised in the house of Madame de Maintenon, and Louis XIV. himself asked some of the courtiers if they had read it.[1] If the upper classes were already familiar with books of this type, certainly the writings of the philosophers were not at all needed to lessen their respect and love for royalty.

If anything was still needed to complete the total discredit into which the royalty had fallen in the eyes of the educated classes, the regency of the Duke of Orleans, with its scandalous orgies, supplied that desideratum long before the advent of Voltaire and Rousseau, Diderot and D'Alembert. The philosophers of the eighteenth century must have been invisibly present in the age of Louis XIV., and even earlier, agitating the upper and educated classes by some mysterious telepathic arrangement, or must have inhabited the bodies of these classes in some supernatural fashion, if we are to suppose that they were the first propagators of revolutionary ideals amongst the nobility and bourgeoisie.

[1] "Memoires de St. Simon" (Hachette, Paris), vol. x., pp. 38, 39.

To those who desire to study the gradual rise of anti-monarchical sentiments amongst the upper classes in France, no book is so enlightening as "D'Argenson's Journal." We can here trace from the commencement how the strong monarchical feelings of the statesman were gradually shaken by the course of events, until in 1759 he writes: "The time for adoration is past, the name of 'Master' so sweet to our ancestors sounds harshly on our ears; I have seen in our times the love and respect of the people towards the King gradually diminishing. From a scuffle they will pass on to revolt, and from revolt to a total revolution. . . ." "Democracy in Monarchy," he said later on, "is the only good government that I can conceive of; these small subordinate democracies will alone find the true equation between the happiness of the people and the glory of princes, between liberty and power." If a defender of the throne, and one of the ablest statesmen of the century, could talk and write in this fashion, we can imagine how the average nobleman or bourgeois of the times must have thought and acted.

Not only so; even amongst the lower classes the spirit of discontent was rife during the past half of the eighteenth century. Saint Simon tells us how, in 1709, there arose popular tumults in

Paris and elsewhere owing to the dearth of bread.[1] Louis XIV. heard the cries of the Versailles mob from his windows. The talk among them was bold and frequent, and through the streets and squares they might be heard uttering violent complaints against the King and the Government. Some of them were patiently exhorting others not to be so tolerant and submissive to a Government which could not make them more miserable. Even women joined the tumult, and it was not suppressed till all their demands for bread and ministerial rearrangements in Paris were satisfied, or at any rate till promises of satisfaction were given.

This spirit of dissatisfaction with the Government was aggravated during the Regency; the disasters following Law's financial experiments gave a fresh occasion to the public to display their hatred for the Government. Tumults broke out in Paris; the corpse of a woman suffocated in the rush on Law's Bank was taken to the window of Louis XV.'s chamber; four more were taken to the Regent's residence; and Law hardly escaped with his life from the clutches of the enraged populace.

The majesty of sovereignty was greatly diminished in the public eyes by the revolting cynicism of the Regent's Court. The constant

[1] Vol. vii., p. 71.

conflicts between the King and the Parlements accustomed the people to look on the throne with indifference, and familiarised them further with the idea of opposition. The conflicts between the religious factions, in which the throne was necessarily mixed up, undermined the religious feelings of the multitude and the value of the sanction which religion leant to the King. In 1740 the cries of "Misery, give us bread!" which irresistibly recall to the mind the October days of 1789, were heard amongst the populace addressed to Louis XV. When, on the occasion of the birth of a son to the Dauphin, celebrated by fêtes in Paris, the King showed himself to the people on the balcony of the Hotel de Ville, not a cheer was raised for him. Even strangers in Paris remarked the ominous silence. In the principal towns in the provinces at the same time threatening placards were seen posted on walls and public places expressing the discontent that prevailed. "We feel," writes D'Argenson, "the growth of a philosophical, anti-monarchical, free-government wind; the idea is current, and possibly the form of government, already in some minds, is to be carried out on the first favourable opportunity."

The discontent of the people lent a willing ear to horrid fables, whose absurdity is not more striking than their cruelty. Wheat was thrown into the Seine by the courtiers to starve the people, and baths of blood were the every-day delight of the King. In 1752, we hear of bands of vagabonds formed around Paris, prepared for war, and harassing the officers of customs. In 1754, one Mandrin, at the head of 150 disciplined men, penetrate by force into the towns of Beaune and Autun, break open the prisons, pillage the public treasury and the shops, and sell the wares contained in the latter.

Was all this discontent against the throne the result of abstract discussions about the natural equality of men? Or did the philosophers themselves lead the popular tumults? And yet, where is the distinction between the Parisian tumult of 1740 and the capture of the Bastille in 1789; between the Versailles mob of 1709 and the Versailles mob of October, 1789; between the vagabonds of 1754 and the vagabonds of 1790? Thus it may be said that a spirit of revolution was long agitating the lower classes in France in the early part of the century, when the philosophers were still rocking in their cradles, or learning their elements of grammar.

There is a remarkable document of 1717 which throws a good deal of light on the fact that we have been trying to illustrate.[1] We refer to

"Memoires," vol. xiii., pp. 430-485.

a memoir addressed to the Duke of Orleans, the Regent of France, by Saint Simon, and published in an appendix to his works. It was addressed to the Regent on the subject of a projected convocation of the States-General of France, and was intended to dissuade him from any such project. Saint Simon endeavoured to show how any such meeting of the States-General at the time would end in weakening the authority of the King, which, as Regent, he was bound to retain intact. The deputies, if convoked, would threaten to usurp the authority for themselves. "Their past and present grievances are a sufficient incentive, and to this will be joined the desire for liberty now so fashionable, and also the desire of each deputy to arrogate the authority to himself, which will be all-powerful in such an assembly."[1] They would know that, if they did not take advantage of the opportunity, their freedom would be lost for ever, and they would therefore talk loudly and vehemently.

As early, therefore, as 1717, it would appear that the convocation of the estates of the kingdom would have been attended with the same consequences as in 1789; and the insight of a statesman of the Regency could read into the immediate future the feature of a

[1] "Memoires," vol. xiii., p. 457.

revolutionary agitation which did not break out till three generations later. Voltaire and the other philosophers of the eighteenth century would then have been regarded as the product of the Revolution, than as the cause of it; and human ingenuity would not have been found wanting to discover in the literary history of the last years of Louis XIV.'s rule some obscure pamphlet writers and miserable satire rhymers who would have been pointed out as the potent authors of the political fermentation.

Even women were not exempt from the influence of this revolutionary and anti-monarchical atmosphere of the early part of the century. We have already seen the Tricoteuses of the Revolutionary drama foreshadowed in the insurrections of 1709 and 1740;[1] the educated women, the leaders of the salons, and the women of high birth who in the seventies and the eighties criticised absolute power as a mortal malady, and desired that the actions of sovereigns should be subjected to the censure of their subjects, might not unreasonably evoke the memory of the intriguing duchesses and marchionesses of Saint Simon's memoirs who could talk philosophically over the affairs of State and the political prejudices of the King. No philosophical husbands or friends existed to infect them with these ideas and culture, no

[1] Taine's "Ancien Régime" (Eng. Trans.), pp. 295, 296.

books like the "Contrat Social" to suggest the nature of the topics of conversation.

But we would now go further, and maintain that this spirit of sedition or disaffection towards the *de facto* regime or government, which the eighteenth century political and philosophical writers are so unreasonably said to have originated and propagated in France, was not peculiar to the bourgeoisie and nobility of the century; it was not peculiar to the Parisian and other city mobs in France, nor peculiar even to the eighteenth century as a whole, but that it was a legacy handed down to Frenchmen from the early stages of the Bourbon rule, a tradition handed down by the history of the past, and that it formed, and continues to form, one of the most salient characteristics of the French city life in general.

The Parisian revolutions during the Hundred Years' War offer to us the prototype of all others. We see even in those early times chiefs of corporations organising themselves "into a commune and seizing the power; they proceed by the method of *Journées*, invade the palace, notify, with arms in hand, as emanating from the people, the will of the band that follows them; they massacre the ministers under the eyes of the prince; they assume the dictatorship and govern by terror."[1] It is already a miniature

[1] A. Sorel: "L'Europe et la Revolution Française," vol. i., p. 202.

history of the Revolution of 1789. Etienne Marcel makes us think of Danton, and Caboche recalls Maillard to the memory. In the sixteenth century the League inextricably weaves together into the fibre of French history religious fanaticism and the spirit of anarchy. It foreshadows the formidable organisation of the Jacobins. Catholicism persecuting the Huguenots is the preparation for the followers of the "Religion of Nature," who were in their own turn to persecute all who did not yield to the times; and it is denounced and feared in the same fashion that Jacobinism was denounced and feared in later times. Saint Simon's denunciation of the League required only to be brought up to date to suit Joseph de Maistre in his polemic against the men of 1793.

Even the Parisian risings have their precedents and classical types. Writing of 1648, Retz remarks · "The movement was like a sudden and violent fire which spread from Pont Neuf through the whole town. Everybody, without exception, took up arms. Children, five or six years old, might be seen with poignards in hand; mothers carried these little ones themselves. There were in Paris twelve hundred barricades at least in two hours, lined with flags and arms. As I was obliged to go out for a moment to appease a tumult in Rue ·Neuve Notre-Dame, I saw, among other things, a lance dragged rather than carried by a boy of eight, which assuredly belonged to the times of the English wars. What was more curious was a polished vermilion-coloured gorget on which was engraved the figure of Henry III.'s assassin, with the inscription underneath, 'Saint Jacques-Clement.'"[1] And what was the rising due to? It owed its outbreak to the imprisonment of a popular minister. The dismissal of Necker was not without its parallel in early French history.

The most remarkable thing about the Parisian tumults was their suddenness. Retz observes that the night before nobody had dreamed of this rising of 1648; a moment was sufficient to do the work. Often during the troublous times of the Fronde do we read in Retz's memoirs of such risings in Paris; the throwing up of barricades was the usual accompaniment, and often during these fights the word "Republic" was heard lightly uttered, but significant in the light of future history. So familiar were these Parisian risings in those times that we learn that the scions of the royal family themselves did not scruple to make use of them for party purposes. Thus March, 1652, saw the outbreak of such a rising at the instance of the King's

[1] *Cf.* "Retz Memoires," vol. ii., p. 62 (Charpentier, Paris, 1859).

brother and M. le Prince. Placards threatening insurrection were posted up, and agitation had already begun near the Pont Neuf, when it suited the purposes of the instigators to disown it; and a few days after the Parlement punished some of the leaders of the rising.

A hundred years later "D'Argenson's Journal" informs us of similar movements as being the commonly expected events of the day—the ordinary conduit pipes of Parisian indignation. In 1720 violent placards had been distributed in Paris and the principal towns—"Kill the tyrant, and do not trouble yourselves further."[1] The Ghost of Ravaillac was frequently exhorted to come back to earth to deliver France from its terrible ogre, and Frenchmen were said to live only to curse and abhor Louis XV.

Voltaire's remark, quoted by Saint Beauve,[2] that Frenchmen are ever ready to pass from the opera to St. Bartholomew, could not have been more happily worded; and the Abbé Martin, talking to Candide, exactly hits off the Frenchman when he observes: "Imagine all possible contradictions and contrasts; you shall see them in the government, in the tribunals, in the churches, in the amusements of this queer

[1] Sorel: *Op. cit.*, vol. i., p. 203.
[2] "St. Beauve Causeries," tom. xii. (Voltaire).

nation. They laugh whilst getting enraged; they groan with the violent outbursts of laughter."

Such was the traditional character of the French populace in those times, a character which it would have retained even if all the philosophers of France had preached against it in their loudest voice and most eloquent language, and a character which it still retains in all its strength. The Frenchmen who one day were ready to die for the King, and shouted at the top of their voices the usual "*Vive le Roi*," and who the next day joined the insurrectionists in the destruction of the Bastille; the Frenchmen who kissed each other as a token of fraternity on the motion of La Mourette, and in a few days were as ready to cut each other's throats; the men who shouted one day with Danton and the next day exulted over his dead body on the guillotine; who were willing to die for the Republic under Robespierre and for the Empire under Napoleon; who raised Napoleon III. to the throne, and cursed him after the Sedan disaster, were the real Frenchmen of history, the true successors of the Parisian democrats of the Fronde. And if we were to be told to-morrow that the Faubourg St. Antoine or the Faubourg St. Denis threw up barricades as they did in the days of the Commune in 1870, and proclaimed themselves in insurrection because President Loubet caused to be scratched out the words, "Liberty, Equality, Fraternity," from the façades of one of the public buildings of Paris, there would be nothing to surprise us in the announcement.

Why then blame the French writers of the eighteenth century for what was in effect one of the essential traits so inherent in the French national temperament? It was the fact that they belonged to the French nation that determined the nature of their writings and of their philosophical views, and not these views that produced the spirit of sedition. The cause, even if it were a *vera causa*, is too inadequate for the effect; and for the explanation of that effect, instead of a solitary writer like Voltaire or Rousseau, or even a group of writers like the Encyclopædists, an intellectual Briarius would be required, working since the times of Charlemagne and Hugh Clovis, and renewing his physical life and intellectual strength every hundred years. And if we could allow ourselves to imitate at a distance the manner of Dr. Pangloss, we might not unreasonably argue in favour of the view that we have been criticising in the following fashion: " Notice that the revolutionary and republican ideas in France in 1789 required that there should have been philosophers who gave rise to them; and hence we have the eighteenth century philosophers. Notice also that the atheism of the Revolution required that there should have been some books to preach atheism, and hence we have the 'System of Nature' and the 'Natural History of the Soul.'"

CHAPTER VIII

FRENCH LITERATURE A REFLECTION OF FRENCH SOCIETY

THERE is another significant fact which is too often forgotten during these days, which is that the actual constitution of French society during the Ancien Régime rendered it necessary that the literary men of the times should reflect the spirit and tone of thought of the upper and educated classes. The highest circles in Paris and France, together with a few of the bourgeoisie, were the only persons who may be called educated, and it was to these only that the philosophers of the Ancien Régime could address themselves. They had no other public to appeal to, and were absolutely dependent on the suffrages of those classes who alone could secure to them praise, honours, rewards.

It was a kind of dependence that the literary history of France amply illustrates for those who care to read it. For a year preceding 1753 the French drama had fallen into disfavour with the general public. The actors, the authors, and the managers perceived the **difficulty of their situation**, and of course considered that something ought to be done to remove the threatening outlook. D'Alembert was induced to compose a brilliant appeal to the public, and Le Kaim read it out from the Théâtre Français. This appeal characteristically emphasises the absolute dependency of the successors of Molière, Corneille, and Racine on the "bounty, the encouragement, and the indulgence" of the audience. It was perhaps an inevitable result of the patronage of French literature by the Court as early as the times of Richelieu.

The foundation of the French Academy marked the first step in this direction, when the able statesman of the times thought he could be the patron of literature and reward merit through the instrumentality of a body of experts. Louis XIV. continued the traditions of Richelieu, and the brilliancy of the age has often been said to be due to the distinguishing mind of the monarch who sought out real merit and encouraged it by liberal donations. Louis XV. was not backward in this connection, and all the public entertainments and fêtes that were given by the Court of Versailles were accompanied by the performance of operas and plays, represented generally for the first time, and never repeated.

The higher nobility followed in the wake of the Court, and the dependence of literature on the upper classes gradually became more complete and inevitable. The tide of literature in Paris ebbed and flowed with the movements of the Court, and it was a commonplace observation that every year the literary activity of Paris was at its highest when the French nobility returned to Paris from Fontainebleau, when authors could win the greatest applause, and booksellers command the greatest sale of their wares. The policy which induced Colbert to engage Pollisson to write a history of Louis XIV. was continued under the Regency; and the French Academy during the course of the eighteenth century became a potent means of supporting literature, through the gifts which it now and again received from private individuals, conferring prizes and endowing chairs. Individual nobles often encouraged the publication of works by rising authors, and partly as a consequence of this encouragement genius degenerated into industry and laborious application, and creative activity into criticism and commonplace reflection. Grimm[1] praised Louis XV. for the support and favourable reception which the monarch gave to literature and philosophy, and said that without such support

[1] "Correspondence," Part II., tom. iii., p. 89.

Frenchmen would not have seen so many literary men flourish in the eighteenth century.

If such was the dependence of the literary men of the times on the upper and educated classes, there could be no wonder if they felt themselves led inevitably to reproduce the thoughts and sentiments of their patrons and friends. We find the Abbé Reynal in 1755 remarking: "It should always be an author's aim to try and know how to please, not the majority of fools who admire every commonplace and insipid work, and lavish the most outrageous epithets of praise on the most undeserving works, but the few wise and enlightened people whose decisions are free from prejudice and always just," and therefore not liable to shift from time to time. About the year 1772 there appeared a periodical publication entitled the *French Spectator*. The author, a M. de La Croix, announced in one of the numbers the purpose and nature of the journal. Being thoroughly acquainted with the tone and manners of his readers, he said: "He will not be found to be sober and taciturn like the English Spectator. He will not fume; he will not be forced to drink; he will be light and affable; his discourses will be gallant rather than profound; his look will penetrate into the hearts of women, and he will be their protector against their husbands." Certainly French society could not have found a more agreeable pamphlet than the *French Spectator*.

The arrival of every foreign prince or scion of royalty in Paris was marked by a visit to the Academy of the Forty Immortals and the sister Academies of the Sciences and Belles Lettres; and the presence of these royal visitors was always an incentive to authors and the men of science to read remarkable papers in the meetings held in their honour. Diderot was in correspondence with Catherine of Russia, and Voltaire was a special favourite with Frederick the Great; and a regular correspondence was carried on between the German patron of French literature and the philosophers at Paris. Literature and philosophy thus became more and more dependent on the support of the upper classes in France as well as the royalty.

Indeed, throughout the history of France we find that the national literature is a faithful echo of the spirit of the times; the causes of this circumstance are to be found in the peculiar temperament of the French nation and in the policy pursued by the Government with reference to literary activity among its subjects. The French Academy has for centuries guided the tastes of the nation, and the peculiar characteristic of French literature has been its social character.

Nothing which does not please the tastes of the literary public has ever a chance of success, and the tastes of that public have always been faithfully represented by the Academy. No French man of genius has therefore ever made a name without adapting himself to the prevailing tone of elegant society. We may be exaggerating this tendency of French literature to a certain extent, but about this general truth there remains no doubt that there has always been an intimate connection—one might say harmony—between the literature of that nation and its literary public.

If from these general considerations we turn to the actual facts of the case, we shall immediately perceive that almost all the distinguishing marks of the literature of the eighteenth century faithfully reproduced the intellectual tone and the practical life of the upper classes.

The first and most obvious characteristic of French literature throughout the century was its anti-Christian attitude. Montesquieu's "Persian Letters" already resound with the echoes of the underground storm which was soon to burst in its full fury. He talks of the "Magician Pope," who forces princes to believe "that the bread which they eat is not bread, or that the wine which they drink is not wine, and a thousand other things of the same nature."[1] "The Christian religion," he says elsewhere,[2] "is loaded with a vast number of difficult practices, and as it is judged less easy to fulfil those obligations than to have bishops to dispense with them, they have, for the public benefit, taken the latter method in such a manner that if they are unwilling to subject themselves to the formalities of marriage, if they would break their vows, if they would marry contrary to the appointment of the law, nay, sometimes, if they are not desirous to abide by their oath, they go to the bishop or pope, who presently grants a dispensation." And speaking of the Spanish intolerance: "When a man comes into the hands of these people there, it is happy for him if he has always prayed to God with little wooden balls in his hands, if he has carried about with him pieces of cloth fastened to two ribbons, and if he has been sometimes in the province of Galicia."

D'Alembert chose the occasion of his election to the French Academy in 1755 to ventilate his views on religion and philosophy; and they met with unprecedented applause and approval. "The birth of the Christian religion," he said, "is the epoch of the decadence of healthy philosophy. The annihilation of philosophy and the progress of religion have always gone together, and the

[1] Letter xxiv. [2] Letter xxix.

moment that saw the establishment of faith in Europe also saw the most complete barbarisation of all the nations." Religion is thus made to serve us only in the other world; and it can do nothing for the advancement of our happiness in this world. For this latter and more laudable task, said D'Alembert, the philosophy of the eighteenth century was alone adequate.

The "System of Nature," now attributed to one author and now to another, which carried out the principles of the sensationalistic philosophy of the times to its logical consequences, and consistently applied the mechanical principles of nature to the phenomena of life and spirit, went even further than D'Alembert. "Theology, with its notions, far from being useful to the human species, is the true source of all those sorrows which affect the earth, of all those errors by which a man is blinded, of those prejudices which benumb mankind, of that ignorance which renders him credulous, of those vices which torment him, of those governments which oppress him."

The author of the "Philosophical Dictionary," under the article Religion, divided it into the Religion of the State, which kept registers of the baptized, and taught good morals to the people, and Theological Religion, "the source of all imaginable follies and disturbances, the parent of fanaticism and civil discord, the enemy of mankind." And elsewhere the same author remarks: "The most absurd of despotisms, the most humiliating for human nature, the most contradictory and the most fatal is that of priests; and of all sacerdotal empires the most criminal is, without contradiction, that of the Christian religion."[1]

The Encyclopædia treated religion from a rationalistic standpoint, and its *beau ideal* was a kind of bare Deism or natural religion—a worship which reason, left to itself and to its own lights, learns "that it must render to the Supreme Being, author and preserver of all the beings that compose the sensible world, so as to love Him, to adore Him, and not to abuse His creatures." The active feeling of love and reverence towards a Being like ourselves in some respects which Christianity preached was to be replaced by the worship of a principle that was only *rational*. The earthquake of Lisbon, which had given Voltaire an opportunity of asking the world where the Moral Being of Christianity had concealed itself, and why He should have allowed such a calamity to occur, was but one of the many instances which the Encyclopædists urged on

[1] Works, vol. xxx., p. 414.

the attention of mankind for discarding the belief in a personal Creator such as Christianity preached.

In the "Conversation of a Philosopher," Crudelli may be taken to represent the views of Diderot on the Christian religion. "Think," says Crudelli to the Marchioness, "how it has created and how it perpetuates in society, between citizens and citizens, in families, amongst neighbours, the strongest and most enduring hatred. Christ said that he had come to separate the husband from the wife, the mother from her children, brother from sister, friend from friend, and this prediction has been only too faithfully accomplished."[1] A little further on in the same dialogue, Diderot compares religion to the institution of marriage, which may bring happiness to some, but may spell mischief to others. "I allow each one to think in his own fashion," says Crudelli, "provided I am allowed to think in my own. Let not those who are free from prejudices be compelled to submit to an imperious Catechism."

Grimm could not have been much prepossessed in favour of Christianity when, speaking of the marvellous doings of Christ, he could play upon the words of Scripture and say that Christ fed five thousand men with five loaves of bread,

[1] Works (1798, Paris), vol. i., pp. 469, 470.

and Brother Lavalette, by a single act of bankruptcy, removed the bread from the mouths of five thousand people. Condorcet's comprehensive scheme of public instruction has not a word to say on the teaching of religious precepts, and the later scepticism of the Third Republic is already found reflected in leaders of French thought like Rousseau and Condorcet, who would exclude the name of God from the teaching of children.

This spirit of irreligion and hostility to Christianity in literature is but the counterpart of the irreligion which was to be found prominent amongst the upper classes of French society. We find this tendency as early as the end of the seventeenth century in the Court of Louis XIV. Saint Simon relates to us an anecdote but too typical of the general atmosphere around the Court and the upper circles. When the Duke of Orleans was going to Spain to rejoin Berwick, Louis XIV. asked him who were to accompany him. Amongst others, Orleans mentioned Fontpertius. "A Jansenist?" asked Louis XIV. "A Jansenist; he does not believe in God." "Is it so?" replied the King. "Then there is no harm. You can take him with you."

But the pleasantries of the Court were not the only evidence of the indifference to religion in those times. The privileges and the rights which Saint Simon says were capable of being enjoyed by the highest ecclesiastical dignitaries of the kingdom are a curious commentary on the religious tendencies of the epoch. "A cardinal has the right to pass his life in gambling, with good cheer, and with the youngest and prettiest ladies; to have his house constituted a centre of fashionable people, where they might resort for their amusement and convenience, to give balls and fêtes, and to display all the luxury and splendour that can serve to flatter and please others—above all, to have no talk about books, or study, or anything ecclesiastical."

The Regency and the reign of Louis XV. were no way behindhand in this respect. As Mr. Lecky remarks, a church in which Dubois was a cardinal, and was unanimously elected by the bishops president of their General Assembly, neither deserved nor obtained respect. Popular canticles of the times sang of the

> "Temps fortune . . .
> Ou la Folie, agitant son grelot,
> D'un pied leger parcourt toute la France,
> Ou nul mortel ne daigne être devot
> Ou l'on fait tout, excepté pénitence."

And Grimm admitted how the rapid spread of

philosophy had pushed religion into the background, and the open defiance of all ceremonial law had accustomed men to do without it. The clergy, on their part, as we have observed, co-operated towards the result. A brief of Benedict XIV. especially authorised Louis of France to allow the representation of Voltaire's Mahomet; and the representative and head of Catholicism thus sanctioned and allied his name with the representative of the anti-Christian agitation in Europe.

When M. Gresset, in the course of an academic address, alluded to the piety of the Bishop of Venice, who, he said, during the course of twenty years never once left his diocese except when attending the Clerical Assemblies, the circumstance was considered to be so unusual as to be received with applause by the audience. Even the French Academy had amongst its members persons like the Abbé de Voisenon, whose chief merit consisted in the publication of obscene and filthy romances and plays. The reply of the worthy curate who was asked whether he thought "That the bishops who insisted so strenuously on religion had much of it themselves," "There may be four or five among them who still believe," is characteristic of the sceptical tone of the higher clergy of the times. M. Auvergne says to M.

de Montlosier in his Memoirs:[1] "I formed for myself a society of priests, some of whom were deists and others open atheists." Some of them in their pulpit utterances struck openly at the See of Rome, and others avoided the name of Christ, and alluded to him as a Christian legislator.[2] We read the same sign of the times in Barbier's chronicle of the reign of Louis XV., when we find the author, a clergyman, following with sympathy the movement of the Encyclo-pædists, and writing: "The greatest sin of the work, perhaps, is some piquant fling at the Jesuits; and if the work mocks at the sacred things of religion, it deserves that mockery a little."

A curious writing is given by Grimm during the course of his correspondence in 1779, which illustrates the irreligion of the clergy themselves. It is a composition traced on Rousseau's door during a period of sickness. It was written in an unknown hand, and it professed to express the opinion entertained of Rousseau by various classes of the French nation. Amongst these we find it stated that the bishops and the higher clergy were proud of Rousseau and eager for his esteem. Whilst the lower clergy, really devoted to the

[1] Vol. i., p. 37.
[2] Taine: "Ancien Régime," pp. 262, 263.

interests of the philosophers, professed in public to denounce him, and longed to pay him their court in private.

The repeated sacrileges that occurred during the reign of Louis XV., when mobs broke into churches and sometimes robbed them of their property, indicate the general indifference to holy things and the want of respect for religion. The great controversies of the seventeenth century on the question of grace degenerated into miserable quarrels of factions. The Molinists intrigued at the Court to undermine the influence of their rivals; the Jansenists excited the Parlements and the populace against the Jesuits; and the large majority of the nation looked on mockingly and indifferently at all this ecclesiastical anarchism. The vexations and persecutions which the ecclesiastics now and then contrived to inflict on the philosophers and leaders of thought caused them to fall into general disfavour; and the expulsion of the Jesuits in 1762 was hailed with joy by the whole nation.

Already Paris seemed to be familiar with a miniature worship of Reason, when, on returning from a successful campaign in Germany, Marshall Saxe received a crown of laurels from the Goddess of Victory in a theatrical gathering. When the place of *Te Deums* and solemn thanksgivings is usurped by actresses dressed up as pagan goddesses, there needs little more to enable us to establish the general indifference to religious interests. Grimm remarks that if in Voltaire's "Tancrède" the death of the hero towards the end had been associated by the author with religious surroundings, and the ceremonies of the Christian Church had been introduced to bring into relief the contrast between religion and love, the representation of the play would have fallen flat on the audience.

Thus it may be truly said that if the eighteenth century literature was strongly affected by an irreligious wave of thought, it was because the upper classes in France whose life it reproduced were themselves irreligious and depraved. When, therefore, it is incessantly urged by writers who might be expected to be well acquainted with their subject, that the French philosophers of the Ancien Régime dealt a blow to the Christian religion, and gave rise to that wave of irreligion which swept over France, it is apparently quite forgotten that long before the writers preached their crusade against orthodoxy, a sceptical tone of thought was to be observed amongst the educated classes, and that the vast majority of the nation entirely out of contact with the literary world were either indifferent to this scepticism or pursued their lives in full belief in the old faith, unaffected by the writings of the philosophers. It is forgotten that as early as the times of Montaigne, remarks were current about devout persons who held up their hands to heaven, but drew them down if there was a prospect of someone thrusting a pike into their side. It is forgotten that the very abbés and cures, who assembled together to enter a solemn protest against the Academy prescribing a prize for an eulogy on Voltaire, were heirs to the general legacy of irreligion, and were ready to throw their ecclesiastical principles to the wind for a seat in the French Academy or a sinecure at Paris.

But this was not the only characteristic of French manners and life that was reproduced by literature. We have already seen how the anti-monarchical doctrines preached by the philosophers were an echo of sentiments expressed long before by the lawyers of the Parlement, by ecclesiastical writers defending a holy empire, a state inspired by the Church and by the spontaneous cries of street mobs during times of insurrection. There is one other characteristic by which French literature is marked in the Ancien Régime, and which is equally to be observed ruling the lives of the upper classes of French society—we mean the immoral tone of French writings, and its counterpart, the degraded life of the aristocracy and the Court.

First, with reference to literature and philosophy, it may be observed that the philosophy popular in the eighteenth century was sensationalistic in its epistemological aspect, and materialistic in its ontology and cosmology. Now it is generally found that a sensationalistic basis in knowledge leads to a theory of hedonism in morals. If the senses and the feelings are the only primary elements in the constitution of the individual, his only idea of happiness would consist in securing for himself the greatest sum of pleasures. A life of pleasures would be the best life under the circumstances; morality and the concepts of morality — duty, obligation, virtue, merit — would be reduced to terms of pleasure and pain; and the individual devoting his life to the welfare of society, sacrificing his interests for the sake of others, and dying to himself that he may live unto Christ—sacrificing his life in order to regain it in a better order of things—would be looked upon as a maniac whose brain was turned like that of the mystics of old, and over whom society should keep a watchful eye.

And such was just the kind of ethical

theory that was preached by the philosophers of the times. It was the basis of the works of La Mettrie and Helvetius, Diderot and D'Holbach, and it was the source of inspiration of the Encyclopædic movement. And just as there was a natural man in a state of warfare for the political theories of Rousseau, and a natural man with sensations and feelings of the most elementary character for the philosophical speculations of Condillac, so there was a natural man with primary instincts and passions on whom the moralist performed his operations, evolving from him the civilised life of modern society. There was as much a natural theory of ethics as there was a theory of *natural rights* in politics, and a theory of *natural*[1] sensations in knowledge. And though in the development of this theory of morals the crude life of pleasures was subordinated to the social affections and the better springs of action, prudence was still the guide for the individual, and all the higher sanctions of morality necessarily disappeared, just as the higher elements in knowledge had disappeared in the speculations about its formation. This theory of morals found its illustration in Diderot's

[1] We hope to be excused for the unwonted use of this word here.

"Supplement to the Travels of Bougainville," where we have the picture of a society in the state of nature, without the refinement of modern civilisation, and with its own notions of sexual morality, so contrary to ours, but depicted as much healthier than the wickedness of refined life.

This hedonistic moralism found itself reflected in all the other writings of the period. It has been very often said that the writings of the century were marked by a looseness of tone unprecedented in French history; and the charge is not very far from being true. Novels and novel-writing in the century degenerated into sensational sketches of dissipated society, and novels of the type of Richardson's "Pamela" and Fielding's "Tom Jones," which had elevated the public taste in England, were replaced in France by romances like "Les Succès d'un Fat" and the "Memoirs of Madame de Blemont." The comedies of Molière were followed by the plays of Favart, and the humour of the "Fourberies de Scapin" by the obscene witticisms of the "Anglais à Bordeaux." Grimm excuses the freedom of writing in his times by saying that it is a sin to which the best minds in all ages have been liable, and that even the Prefect of Hell will not be too severe on them, considering the good works that at the same time they have left behind them.

The publication of Saint Simon's Memoirs in the early part of the century had prepared the way for a host of others, where the most disgusting jests were often made at the expense of the Court or private individuals. The Parisian of the Third Republic who finds such pleasure in reading in the daily papers the scandalous antecedents of the lives of French statesmen hunted up with the greatest care, or manufactured when there was nothing to hunt up, had his prototype in the Parisian of the Ancien Régime, who could delight in these plays and comedies which made indirect allusions to the lives of the people belonging to the Court, and of which there were to be found large numbers on the stage.

This immoral tone of literature was supplemented by the immoral and licentious life generally led by the Court and the nobility, from which even the clergy were not free. The early years of the Regency and the orgies of the Duke of Orleans have become a commonplace in French history. An immoderate and selfish love of pleasure, so strongly defended by the philosophy of the day, characterised the nobility of the Ancien Régime. The Court of Louis XV., a prince educated under such good guidance as that of a Jesuit father and the dissolute head of the Regency, became a by-word in history for corruption and immorality. The Queen of France could freely join in the intrigues of her waiting-maids and Court ladies, and add postscripts in verse to the criminal love-letters of her companions. The mistresses of the King freely sold the highest offices in the kingdom to their relations and paramours; the administration of the kingdom became a host of sinecures for the maintenance of worthless and incapable flatterers; and the gaiety of Versailles passed into a proverbial expression for a life of dissolute pleasures.

The melancholy "Histoire de Geneviève," written by a lady of the Court, may not inaptly be said to represent in miniature the degeneracy in morals which had crept over the better classes of Frenchmen in the Ancien Régime. Grimm relates to us how, one day in 1780, when the King was attending a play at the Comédie Française, some of the leaders of the nobility contrived to carry out a pantomime in the fashion of the Rape of the Sabines. All the actresses of the theatre were suddenly seized and carried away to the house of Mademoiselle R. The motive was alleged to be that a high personage was desirous of demonstrating to his companions some judgment that he had formed with regard to the beauty of one of the actresses.[1] Such were the usual pranks of the French nobility, and they were considered as a matter of course, without casting the least blame on the persons who indulged in them.

The life of Paris was admirably caricatured in one of the pamphlets of the day in a scene between an old man over eighty and an old and blind lady, of nearly the same age, who had lived with him in one of the scandalous connections which were the order of the day in Paris and France. The conversation turned on their long-retained friendship, and the old man remarked: "Yes, there are few connections so old as ours." "Yes, over fifty years." "And in this long interval not a single cloud to disturb our tranquillity." "Yes," replied the lady, "that is what I admire most. But may it not be that this is due to our being indifferent to each other at bottom?" "That is possible."[2]

Even the clergy were not exempt from this whirl of scepticism and moral degradation. Reynal tells us in his correspondence how Diderot once met a curé from Mont Chauvet, who desired to consult him on a madrigal of

[1] Grimm: "Correspondence," Part II., tom. v., p. 216.
[2] Grimm, Part II., tom. iv., pp. 273, 274.

700 lines composed by him, and suggested, the curé said, by a curious domestic incident. The incident referred to a scandalous intrigue of his valet with one of his female servants, which resulted in adding one more to the total number of the nation. The society of those times was quite familiar with men of the type of Abbé Voisenon, who passed his life alternately between his confessor, P. St. Jean, and Mademoiselle Favart of the Italian Comedy, and who wrote with "reluctance and remorse" works whose obscenity was not any way far behind the general degradation of the upper classes. It was quite familiar with the saintly leaders of a straying flock, like the Abbé Galiani, who wrote, in his correspondence with Madame D'Epinay: " Can the mind stand any favourable comparison with the stomach?"

The literature of the century, therefore, was throughout a faithful representation of the dissolute life and manners of the nation, and what the upper classes did and deserved, it was necessary that literature should justify and confirm. The composition of the "Pucelle" could only have belonged to a time like that of the Orleans Regency, and its reception could have been favourable only with the courtiers and nobility of the Saint Simon type. So, likewise, in the latter years of the Ancien Régime, a society in which Madame D'Epinay's gallant sat at table with her husband, with the latter's complete permission, and in which M. D'Epinay referred in his wife's presence to his notorious relations with two public women, in which an opera dancer could preside at the table of a patrician abbé, found itself faithfully reflected in works like Duclos's "Histoire de la Baronne de Luz."

In short, a kind of destruction of family life may be said to have gradually crept in amongst the nobility and the better classes of France, which was a certain index to the misfortunes of the nation. The invidious distinction between the rich and the poor, the inequality of fortunes—luxury on the one side and extreme misery on the other—all these may be said to have followed in the wake of the degeneration of family life amongst the upper classes. And it is this same degeneration that expresses itself in the loose tone of the writings of the period. The low canaille, the rabble which afterwards took such a leading part in the Revolution, did not owe their rise to the fulminations of the writers against monarchy, but to the harsh, insensible, perverted nobility, who neglected the interests of the poor, and allowed them to pass over from a life of honesty into a life of helplessness, idleness, and finally discontent. It was not the literary, but the social factor, which we have just indicated, that was the potent motive-power to the outbreak of revolutionary anarchy in 1789 and the succeeding years. And the writers who have been so often denounced as the authors and preachers of political anarchism were but the passive instruments in the hands of a destiny that hurried them on in the general current of the age.

There was another characteristic of the literature of the Ancien Régime which deserves to be considered shortly. We have already had occasion to allude to the sanguine aspirations of the authors of the times with regard to the future of the human race, and the healthy optimism which refused to believe in doctrines like that of essential corruption and evil in man. It was this faith in the perfectibility of man that was the indispensable basis of the movement of the Encyclopædia. It was this that inspired those heroic bands of writers to struggle against overwhelming difficulties and the insults of their enemies. It was this that led Rousseau to denounce the products of modern civilisation, and to figure a new era in the history of nations, when the individual could develop according to the principles of nature. We all remember the dazzling sketch which Condorcet wrote during the later years of his life, and which he finished a few moments before his cruel end. The truth, embodied in Wordsworth's famous lines:

> "I have heard of hearts unkind, kind deeds
>   With coldness still returning;
> Alas! the gratitude of men
>   Has oftener left me mourning,"

was repeated in a thousand forms and places by the writers of the eighteenth century.

Even the Catholic clergy, the people who had most to suffer from this faith in the material perfectibility of men and the consequent thirst for knowledge, found themselves unable to resist the general impetus, and were carried away in the general vortex. They endeavoured to edit the volumes of the Encyclopædia from their own standpoint after having induced the King to order the suppression of the first volumes, and to persecute the organisers of the work. Many a bold plan was suggested and put into execution during the course of the century for the spread of scientific and historic information among the people; and amongst the most remarkable of such schemes may be mentioned that of Reynal in 1754, which aimed at establishing a monthly journal in France, having six editors of the best culture travelling over different places in Europe, and communicating their experiences to Frenchmen through their journal.

This optimistic tone of literature reflected the one healthy side of the better class of Frenchmen that still remained. Corresponding to this side we have the Choiseuls and the **Turgots, the Mouniers** and the Mirabeaus of the eighteenth century—men who had shaken themselves free from the degradation of the times, and were bent on regenerating French society without the aid of the Revolutionary terror.

The French literature of the eighteenth century, therefore, was but the reflected image of the life and modes of thinking, of the religious and social tendencies of the upper and educated classes of France. If it was irreligious and sceptical, it was because French society was so; if it was anti-monarchical or republican in politics, it was because the French society of those times was already anti-monarchical in views, **if not in practice.** The ordinary intellect guided by historians has often believed in the usual charges against the philosophers of the Ancien Régime, much in the fashion of the traveller in the fable who, being constantly told that he was carrying a **pig** on his back, came to believe in it, **and** threw down the goat on the road. But a closer study of the period would suffice to prove to his satisfaction the falsehood of an unconscious misrepresentation of facts, if not of an interested fable.

CHAPTER IX

CONCLUSION

HERE we must conclude. Of late there has been a tendency to question the traditional acceptation of the term "French Revolution," and to understand by the words only the principles of 1789, and the attempts made to realise them in practice. We welcome such a tendency as part of the general attempt at forming a philosophy of history; but it will not affect the position we have taken up with regard to the philosophers. The principles of 1789 were both destructive and constructive, and we have endeavoured to demonstrate that the philosophers of the Ancien Régime were the exponents of the spirit of the times, with reference to the destructive as well as the constructive aspect. Instead of being so many prophets and preachers of a new gospel, they were the priests, as it were, of the Genius of the French Nobility and Bourgeoisie who gave forth to the world the inspirations of their Master.

It is possible that the extremely popular form of their writings, their simplicity of style, and clearness of thinking, may have facilitated the rapid spread of revolutionary ideals among the masses; but the ground was long before prepared, and the train long before laid for the bursting of the explosion. When, indeed, a series of circumstances led to the establishment of a republic in France in 1792, the men who were pushed forward, as it were, to the helm of affairs, tried to put into practice some of the principles and ideas of the eighteenth century philosophers. A large majority of the Girondists would have carried out the principles of the "Héloïse" and the "Émile" if they could. Danton was a disciple of Diderot, and Robespierre and his party the worshippers of the real Rousseau—the Rousseau of the "Social Compact" theory, the principles of which inspired the Constitution of 1793. The sovereignty of the State and the annihilation of all individual liberty in that sovereignty were realised in the Reign of Terror, as the principle of individual liberty of the "Contrat Social" would have been realised in the Constitutional Monarchy of 1791. And as if to complete all, we have the frightful logic of De Sade reflected in the croakings of Marat and the *noyades* and *fusillades* of Carrière and his colleagues; the licentious brutality and speculative anarchy of the French writers find a corollary in the revolting atrocities of the Jacobin despotism.

But the atrocities and terror would still have been there; the sovereignty of the people, which really amounted to the sovereignty of the ignorant, illiterate, impulsive, hungry, and passionate mob of Paris and the faubourges, would still have been asserted, and the anarchy would not have been mitigated by the difference of a hair's-breadth, even if Rousseau had not written his "Social Compact," and the Encyclopædia had been crushed in the bud by the efforts of the Jesuits. The mobs that gathered at Paris on the 14th of July and the 10th of August would not have gathered the less, even if the revolutionary writings had been transformed by an invisible hand into docile flattery of the Monarchy; the September Massacres would not have been prevented if Voltaire had preached himself hoarse as the staunchest defender of the Catholic Faith. The traditions of centuries would not have been forgotten in the absence of the philosophic propaganda; and Frenchmen would not have been less of Frenchmen because Rousseau and Diderot and D'Alembert were silent or tame.

It is now time we closed this essay. The opinion that was pronounced on the influence of these writers as the originators of the Revolution by Comte in the early part of the last century has been confirmed by the late English historian of the eighteenth century. Mr. Lecky remarks about the greatest of these writers—Rousseau—" The works of Rousseau contain much that is utterly and irreconcilably opposed to the Revolution,"[1] and about the eighteenth century philosophers in general, that it is time that historians left off the commonplaces about the philosophers being the cause of the movement of 1789. The first judgment of history is very often the last; and the judgment that inspired the famous preface to the Encyclopædia is just the judgment that makes the latest French historian of the century—M. A. Sorel—remark: "The French philosophers did not create the causes of the Revolution; they only manifested them."

[1] " History of the Eighteenth Century," vol. v., p. 360 *et seq.*

INDEX

Academy, The, 99.
Adams, G. B., 15, "Growth of the French Nation."
"Ancien Régime," The, 17, 18, 20, 29, 30, 42, 43, 76, 95, 124.
Aulard, 19, "Histoire Politique de la Rev. Fr."
Auvergne, 108, "Memoirs."

Bacon, 47, 48.
Barbier, 108, "Reign of Louis XV."
Bayle, 68.
Bossuet, 48.
Brougham, Lord, 13.
Bruno, Giordano, 47.
Burke, 13.
Buzot, 27.

Caboche, 89.
"Cahiers," The, 19.
Calas, 26, 38, 74.
Calvinists, The, 74.
Campanella, 48.
Carrière, 125.
Cartesian School, The, 55.
Cerutti, 42.
Charron, 48.
Chateaubriand, 27.
Choiseul, 122.
Comte, 49, 126.
Condillac, 54, 113.
Condorcet, 22, 30, 40, 42, 64, 105, 106, 121.
"Contrat Social." See *Rousseau*.
Corneille, 48, 57.
Crebillon, 57.
Crudelli, 104, "Conversation of a Philosopher."

Daniel, P., 80, "History of France."
Danton, 31, 89, 92, 125.
D'Alembert, 27, 81, 96, 102, 103, 126, "Elements of Philosophy"; "Candide," 62, 91.
D'Argenson, 22, 82, 84, 91, "Journal."
De Bonald, 11.
De la Croix, 98.
D'Epinay, Madame, 119.
De Maistre, 11, 89.
De Sade, 125.
Desmoulins, Camille, 14, 31.
Descartes, 48, 54.
Diderot, 14, 23, 41, 58, 64, 67, 81, 99, 104, 113, 117, 125, 126; "Furieux de la Liberté," 23; "Merit and Virtue," 67.
Ducos, 53, "History of Louis XIV. and XV."
Duke of Orleans, 19, 69, 81, 86, 105, 115.

Encyclopædia, The, 9, 23, 24, 39, 40, 41, 58, 60, 64, 80, 93, 103, 121, 126.

Favart, 114.
Fenelon, 48.
Ficino, 45.

Galiani, Abbé, 118.
Girondists, The, 125.
Grant, A. J., 34, "French Monarchy."
Gresset, 57, 107.

130 Index

Grimm, 10, 11, 25, 28, 51, 97, 104, 106, 109, 110, 114, 117, "Correspondence."
Goethe, 16.

Hanotaux, 78, "Histoire de Cardinal Richelieu."
Harrison, Frederic, 16, "What 1789 did."
Helvetius, 22, 42, 61, 69, 113; "L'Esprit," 42, 61.
"Histoire de Geneviève," 116.
Hobbes, 72.
Holbach, 41, 67, 68, 69, 71, 113.
Hotman, 78, "Franco Gallia."

Jacobins, 12, 89, 125.
Jansenists, 74, 105, 109.
Jaucourt, Chevalier de, 58.
Jesuits, 74, 109, 126.

Kuno Fischer, 45, "Descartes and his School."
Kant, 48.

La Barre, 38, 74.
La Boëtie, 78.
La Mettrie, 54, 64, 66, 67, 113.
Lafayette, 31.
Languet, Hubert, 78, "Vindiciæ contra Tyrannos."
Lavalette, 105.
Law's Bank, 83.
Le Franc de Pompignan, 11.
Lecky, 106, 127.
Lilly, W. S., 16.
Louis XIV., 21, 48, 77, 79, 81, 83, 87, 96.
Louis XV., 15, 25, 77, 83, 84, 91, 96, 106, 109, 115.
Louis XVI., 9, 21, 30, 31.
Lytton, Lord, 14.

Mably, 53, "History of France."
Machiavelli, 45.
Maillard, 89.
Malebranche, 55.
Marat, 14, 125.

Marcel, Etienne, 89.
Marmontel, 56, "Poétique Française."
Maury, Abbé, 19.
Michael Angelo, 45.
Michelet, 12.
Minden, 10.
Mirabeau, 30, 42, 122.
Molière, 48, 57, 114; "Femmes Savantes," 57.
Molinists, The, 110.
Montaigne, 48.
Montesquieu, 20, 21, 24, 36, 40; "Esprit des Lois," 20, 25, 37, 42, 72, 80; "Supplement to the Age of Louis XIV.," 21; "Lettres Persanes," 37, 70, 101; "Considerations on the Decay of the Romans," 37.
Montlosier, 108.
Morellet, 40.
Morley, John, 14.
Mounier, 13, 42, 122.

Necker, 90.

Palissot, 10.
Papists, The, 74.
Paracelsus, 45.
"Philosophical Dictionary," The, 102.
"Physiocrats," The, 60.
Piron, 57.
Pollisson, 97, "History of Louis XIV."
"Pucelle," The, 118.

Racine, 49, 57.
Raphael, 57.
Reformation, The, 46, 47, 68.
Renaissance, The, 45, 47, 48, 49.
Retz, 89, 90, "Memoires."
"Revolutionary Man," The, 11.
Reynal, Abbé, 29, 42, 80, 98; "History of the Indies," 52.
Richelieu, 77, 78.
Robespierre, 31, 125.
Rosbach, 10.

Index

Rose, J. H., 15.
Rousseau, 9, 11, 12, 14, 15, 22, 26, 29, 32, 38, 39, 40, 41, 63, 64, 73, 74, 81, 93, 105, 108, 125; "Contrat Social," 12, 25, 26, 40, 78, 88, 125, 126; "Discourse on the Origin of Inequality," 27; "The Dijon Discourse," 32, 40, 80; "Letter on Music," 32; Article, *Political Economy*, in Encyclopædia, 39; "Nouvelle Héloïse," 125; "Émile," 125.

Saint Beauve, 91, "Causeries."
Saint Just, 11.
Saint Simon, 79, 81, 82, 86, 87, 106, "Memoires."
Saxe, Marshall, 109.
Sieyès, 42.
Sorel, A., 88, 91, 127, "L'Europe et la Rev. Fr."
Spinoza, 48.

Sybel, 44, "French Revolution."
"System of Nature," 102.

Taine, 12, 87, 108, "Ancien Régime."
Telesio, 45.
Tollendal, Lally, 27.
Turgot, 21, 24, 29, 30, 33, 40, 122.

Vannini, 47.
Velly, Abbé, 52.
Vergennes, 29.
Victor Hugo, 12.
Voisenon, Abbé, 107, 108.
Voltaire, 9, 11, 12, 14, 15, 20, 21, 22, 29, 37, 53, 57, 59, 62, 63, 69, 72, 80, 81, 91, 93, 99, 103, 126; "History of Charles XII," 52; "Age of Louis XIV," 53; "Morals, Manners and Character of Nations," 53; "Idées Republicaines," 73; Tancrède, 110.

Printed by Cowan & Co., Limited, Perth.

SOCIAL SCIENCE SERIES.

SCARLET CLOTH, EACH 2s. 6d.

1. **Work and Wages.** Prof. J. E. THOROLD ROGERS.
   "Nothing that Professor Rogers writes can fail to be of interest to thoughtful people."—*Athenæum.*

2. **Civilisation: its Cause and Cure.** EDWARD CARPENTER.
   "No passing piece of polemics, but a permanent possession."—*Scottish Review.*

3. **Quintessence of Socialism.** Dr. SCHÄFFLE.
   "Precisely the manual needed. Brief, lucid, fair and wise."—*British Weekly.*

4. **Darwinism and Politics.** D. G. RITCHIE, M.A. (Oxon.).
   New Edition, with two additional Essays on HUMAN EVOLUTION.
   "One of the most suggestive books we have met with."—*Literary World.*

5. **Religion of Socialism.** E. BELFORT BAX.

6. **Ethics of Socialism.** E. BELFORT BAX.
   "Mr. Bax is by far the ablest of the English exponents of Socialism."—*Westminster Review.*

7. **The Drink Question.** Dr. KATE MITCHELL.
   "Plenty of interesting matter for reflection."—*Graphic.*

8. **Promotion of General Happiness.** Prof. M. MACMILLAN.
   "A reasoned account of the most advanced and most enlightened utilitarian doctrine in a clear and readable form."—*Scotsman.*

9. **England's Ideal, &c.** EDWARD CARPENTER.
   "The literary power is unmistakable, their freshness of style, their humour, and their enthusiasm."—*Pall Mall Gazette.*

10. **Socialism in England.** SIDNEY WEBB, LL.B.
    "The best general view of the subject from the modern Socialist side."—*Athenæum.*

11. **Prince Bismarck and State Socialism.** W. H. DAWSON.
    "A succinct, well-digested review of German social and economic legislation since 1870."—*Saturday Review.*

12. **Godwin's Political Justice (On Property).** Edited by H. S. SALT.
    "Shows Godwin at his best; with an interesting and informing introduction."—*Glasgow Herald.*

13. **The Story of the French Revolution.** E. BELFORT BAX.
    "A trustworthy outline."—*Scotsman.*

14. **The Co-Operative Commonwealth.** LAURENCE GRONLUND.
    "An independent exposition of the Socialism of the Marx school."—*Contemporary Review.*

15. **Essays and Addresses.** BERNARD BOSANQUET, M.A. (Oxon.).
    "Ought to be in the hands of every student of the Nineteenth Century spirit."—*Echo.*
    "No one can complain of not being able to understand what Mr. Bosanquet means."—*Pall Mall Gazette.*

16. **Charity Organisation.** C. S. LOCH, Secretary to Charity Organisation Society.
    "A perfect little manual."—*Athenæum.*
    "Deserves a wide circulation."—*Scotsman.*

17. **Thoreau's Anti-Slavery and Reform Papers.** Edited by H. S. SALT.
    "An interesting collection of essays."—*Literary World.*

18. **Self-Help a Hundred Years Ago.** G. J. HOLYOAKE.
    "Will be studied with much benefit by all who are interested in the amelioration of the condition of the poor."—*Morning Post.*

19. **The New York State Reformatory at Elmira.** ALEXANDER WINTER.
    With Preface by HAVELOCK ELLIS.
    "A valuable contribution to the literature of penology."—*Black and White.*

SOCIAL SCIENCE SERIES—(Continued).

20. Common Sense about Women. T. W. HIGGINSON.
"An admirable collection of papers, advocating in the most liberal spirit the emancipation of women."—*Woman's Herald.*

21. The Unearned Increment. W. H. DAWSON.
"A concise but comprehensive volume."—*Echo.*

22. Our Destiny. LAURENCE GRONLUND.
"A very vigorous little book, dealing with the influence of Socialism on morals and religion."—*Daily Chronicle.*

23. The Working-Class Movement in America.
Dr. EDWARD and E. MARX AVELING.
"Will give a good idea of the condition of the working classes in America, and of the various organisations which they have formed."—*Scots Leader.*

24. Luxury. Prof. EMILE DE LAVELEYE.
"An eloquent plea on moral and economical grounds for simplicity of life."—*Academy.*

25. The Land and the Labourers. Rev. C. W. STUBBS, M.A.
"This admirable book should be circulated in every village in the country."—*Manchester Guardian.*

26. The Evolution of Property. PAUL LAFARGUE.
"Will prove interesting and profitable to all students of economic history."—*Scotsman.*

27. Crime and its Causes. W. DOUGLAS MORRISON.
"Can hardly fail to suggest to all readers several new and pregnant reflections on the subject."—*Anti-Jacobin.*

28. Principles of State Interference. D. G. RITCHIE, M.A.
"An interesting contribution to the controversy on the functions of the State."—*Glasgow Herald.*

29. German Socialism and F. Lassalle. W. H. DAWSON.
"As a biographical history of German Socialistic movements during this century it may be accepted as complete."—*British Weekly.*

30. The Purse and the Conscience. H. M. THOMPSON, B.A. (Cantab.).
"Shows common sense and fairness in his arguments."—*Scotsman.*

31. Origin of Property in Land. FUSTEL DE COULANGES. Edited, with an Introductory Chapter on the English Manor, by Prof. W. J. ASHLEY, M.A.
"His views are clearly stated, and are worth reading."—*Saturday Review.*

32. The English Republic. W. J. LINTON. Edited by KINETON PARKES.
"Characterised by that vigorous intellectuality which has marked his long life of literary and artistic activity."—*Glasgow Herald.*

33. The Co-Operative Movement. BEATRICE POTTER.
"Without doubt the ablest and most philosophical analysis of the Co-Operative Movement which has yet been produced."—*Speaker.*

34. Neighbourhood Guilds. Dr. STANTON COIT.
"A most suggestive little book to anyone interested in the social question."—*Pall Mall Gazette.*

35. Modern Humanists. J. M. ROBERTSON.
"Mr. Robertson's style is excellent—nay, even brilliant—and his purely literary criticisms bear the mark of much acumen."—*Times.*

36. Outlooks from the New Standpoint. E. BELFORT BAX.
"Mr. Bax is a very acute and accomplished student of history and economics."—*Daily Chronicle.*

37. Distributing Co-Operative Societies. Dr. LUIGI PIZZAMIGLIO. Edited by F. J. SNELL.
"Dr. Pizzamiglio has gathered together and grouped a wide array of facts and statistics, and they speak for themselves."—*Speaker.*

38. Collectivism and Socialism. By A. NAQUET. Edited by W. HEAFORD.
"An admirable criticism by a well-known French politician of the New Socialism of Marx and Lassalle."—*Daily Chronicle.*

SOCIAL SCIENCE SERIES—(*Continued*).

39. **The London Programme.** SIDNEY WEBB, LL.B.
 "Brimful of excellent ideas."—*Anti-Jacobin*.
40. **The Modern State.** PAUL LEROY BEAULIEU.
 "A most interesting book; well worth a place in the library of every social inquirer."—*N. B. Economist*.
41. **The Condition of Labour.** HENRY GEORGE.
 "Written with striking ability, and sure to attract attention."—*Newcastle Chronicle*.
42. **The Revolutionary Spirit preceding the French Revolution.**
 FELIX ROCQUAIN. With a Preface by Professor HUXLEY.
 'The student of the French Revolution will find in it an excellent introduction to the study of that catastrophe."—*Scotsman*.
43. **The Student's Marx.** EDWARD AVELING, D.Sc.
 "One of the most practically useful of any in the Series."—*Glasgow Herald*.
44. **A Short History of Parliament.** B. C. SKOTTOWE, M.A. (Oxon.).
 "Deals very carefully and completely with this side of constitutional history."—*Spectator*.
45. **Poverty: Its Genesis and Exodus.** J. G. GODARD.
 "He states the problems with great force and clearness."—*N. B Economist*.
46. **The Trade Policy of Imperial Federation.** MAURICE H. HERVEY.
 "An interesting contribution to the discussion."—*Publishers' Circular*.
47. **The Dawn of Radicalism.** J. BOWLES DALY, LL.D.
 "Forms an admirable picture of an epoch more pregnant, perhaps, with political instruction than any other in the world's history."—*Daily Telegraph*.
48. **The Destitute Alien in Great Britain.** ARNOLD WHITE; MONTAGUE CRACKANTHORPE, Q.C.; W. A. M'ARTHUR, M.P.; W. H. WILKINS, &c.
 "Much valuable information concerning a burning question of the day."—*Times*.
49. **Illegitimacy and the Influence of Seasons on Conduct.**
 ALBERT LEFFINGWELL, M.D.
 We have not often seen a work based on statistics which is more continuously interesting."—*Westminster Review*.
50. **Commercial Crises of the Nineteenth Century.** H. M. HYNDMAN.
 "One of the best and most permanently useful volumes of the Series."—*Literary Opinion*.
51. **The State and Pensions in Old Age.** J. A. SPENDER and ARTHUR ACLAND, M.P.
 "A careful and cautious examination of the question."—*Times*.
52. **The Fallacy of Saving.** JOHN M. ROBERTSON.
 "A plea for the reorganisation of our social and industrial system."—*Speaker*.
53. **The Irish Peasant.** ANON.
 'A real contribution to the Irish Problem by a close, patient and dispassionate investigator."—*Daily Chronicle*.
54. **The Effects of Machinery on Wages.** Prof. J. S. NICHOLSON, D.Sc.
 "Ably reasoned, clearly stated, impartially written."—*Literary World*.
55. **The Social Horizon.** ANON.
 "A really admirable little book, bright, clear, and unconventional."—*Daily Chronicle*.
56. **Socialism, Utopian and Scientific.** FREDERICK ENGELS.
 "The body of the book is still fresh and striking."—*Daily Chronicle*.
57. **Land Nationalisation.** A. R. WALLACE.
 "The most instructive and convincing of the popular works on the subject."—*National Reformer*.
58. **The Ethic of Usury and Interest.** Rev. W. BLISSARD.
 "The work is marked by genuine ability."—*North British Agriculturalist*.
59. **The Emancipation of Women.** ADELE CREPAZ.
 "By far the most comprehensive, luminous, and penetrating work on this question that I have yet met with."—*Extract from Mr.* GLADSTONE'S *Preface*.
60. **The Eight Hours' Question.** JOHN M. ROBERTSON.
 "A very cogent and sustained argument on what is at present the unpopular side."—*Times*.
61. **Drunkenness.** GEORGE R. WILSON, M.B.
 "Well written, carefully reasoned, free from cant, and full of sound sense."—*National Observer*.
62. **The New Reformation.** RAMSDEN BALMFORTH.
 "A striking presentation of the nascent religion, how best to realize the personal and social ideal."—*Westminster Review*.
63. **The Agricultural Labourer.** T. E. KEBBEL.
 "A short summary of his position, with appendices on wages, education, allot-

SOCIAL SCIENCE SERIES—(Continued).

65. **England's Foreign Trade in XIXth Century.** A. L. BOWLEY.
   "Full of valuable information, carefully compiled."—*Times.*
66. **Theory and Policy of Labour Protection.** Dr. SCHÄFFLE.
   "An attempt to systematise a conservative programme of reform."—*Man. Guard.*
67. **History of Rochdale Pioneers.** G. J. HOLYOAKE.
   "Brought down from 1844 to the Rochdale Congress of 1892."—*Co-Op. News.*
68. **Rights of Women.** M. OSTRAGORSKI.
   "An admirable storehouse of precedents, conveniently arranged."—*Daily Chron.*
69. **Dwellings of the People.** LOCKE WORTHINGTON.
   "A valuable contribution to one of the most pressing problems of the day."—*Daily Chronicle.*
70. **Hours, Wages, and Production.** Dr. BRENTANO.
   "Characterised by all Professor Brentano's clearness of style."—*Economic Review.*
71. **Rise of Modern Democracy.** CH. BORGEAUD.
   "A very useful little volume, characterised by exact research."—*Daily Chronicle.*
72. **Land Systems of Australasia.** WM. EPPS.
   "Exceedingly valuable at the present time of depression and difficulty."—*Scots. Mag.*
73. **The Tyranny of Socialism.** YVES GUYOT. Pref. by J. H. LEVY.
   "M. Guyot is smart, lively, trenchant, and interesting."—*Daily Chronicle.*
74. **Population and the Social System.** Dr. NITH.
   "A very valuable work of an Italian economist."—*West. Rev.*
75. **The Labour Question.** T. G. SPYERS.
   "Will be found extremely useful."—*Times.*
76. **British Freewomen.** C. C. STOPES.
   "The most complete study of the Women's Suffrage question."—*English Wom. Rev.*
77. **Suicide and Insanity.** Dr. J. K. STRAHAN.
   "An interesting monograph dealing exhaustively with the subject."—*Times.*
78. **A History of Tithes.** Rev. H. W. CLARKE.
   "May be recommended to all who desire an accurate idea of the subject."—*D. Chron.*
79. **Three Months in a Workshop.** P. GOHRE, with Pref. by Prof. ELY.
   "A vivid picture of the state of mind of German workmen."—*Manch. Guard.*
80. **Darwinism and Race Progress.** Prof. J. B. HAYCRAFT.
   "An interesting subject treated in an attractive fashion."—*Glasgow Herald.*
81. **Local Taxation and Finance.** G. H. BLUNDEN.
82. **Perils to British Trade.** E. BURGIS.
83. **The Social Contract.** J. J. ROUSSEAU. Edited by H. J. TOZER.
84. **Labour upon the Land.** Edited by J. A. HOBSON, M.A.
85. **Moral Pathology.** ARTHUR E. GILES, M.D., B.Sc.
86. **Parasitism, Organic and Social.** MASSART and VANDERVELDE.
87. **Allotments and Small Holdings.** J. L. GREEN.
88. **Money and its Relations to Prices.** L. L. PRICE.
89. **Sober by Act of Parliament.** F. A. MACKENZIE.
90. **Workers on their Industries.** F. W. GALTON.
91. **Revolution and Counter-Revolution.** KARL MARX.
92. **Over-Production and Crises.** K. RODBERTUS.
93. **Local Government and State Aid.** S. J. CHAPMAN.
94. **Village Communities in India.** B. H. BADEN-POWELL, M.A., C.I.E.
95. **Anglo-American Trade.** S. J. CHAPMAN.
96. **A Plain Examination of Socialism.** GUSTAVE SIMONSON, M.A., M.D.
97. **Commercial Federation & Colonial Trade Policy.** J. DAVIDSON, M.A., Phil.D.
98. **Selections from Fourier.** C. GIDE and J. FRANKLIN.
99. **Public-House Reform.** A. N. CUMMING.
100. **The Village Problem.** G. F. MILLIN.
101. **Toward the Light.** L. H. BERENS.
102. **Christian Socialism in England.** A. V. WOODWORTH.

DOUBLE VOLUMES, 3s. 6d.

1. **Life of Robert Owen.** LLOYD JONES.
2. **The Impossibility of Social Democracy: a Second Part of "The Quintessence of Socialism".** Dr. A. SCHÄFFLE.
3. **Condition of the Working Class in England in 1844.** FREDERICK ENGELS.
4. **The Principles of Social Economy.** YVES GUYOT.
5. **Social Peace.** G. VON SCHULTZE-GAEVERNITZ.
6. **A Handbook of Socialism.** W. D. P. BLISS.
7. **Socialism: its Growth and Outcome.** W. MORRIS and E. B. BAX.

CPSIA information can be obtained
at www.ICGtesting.com
Printed in the USA
LVOW13s0917240617
539247LV00010B/547/P